SOUTH AMERICA

| PHYSICAL FEATURES | POLITICAL DIVISIONS | RESOURCES | CULTURE |

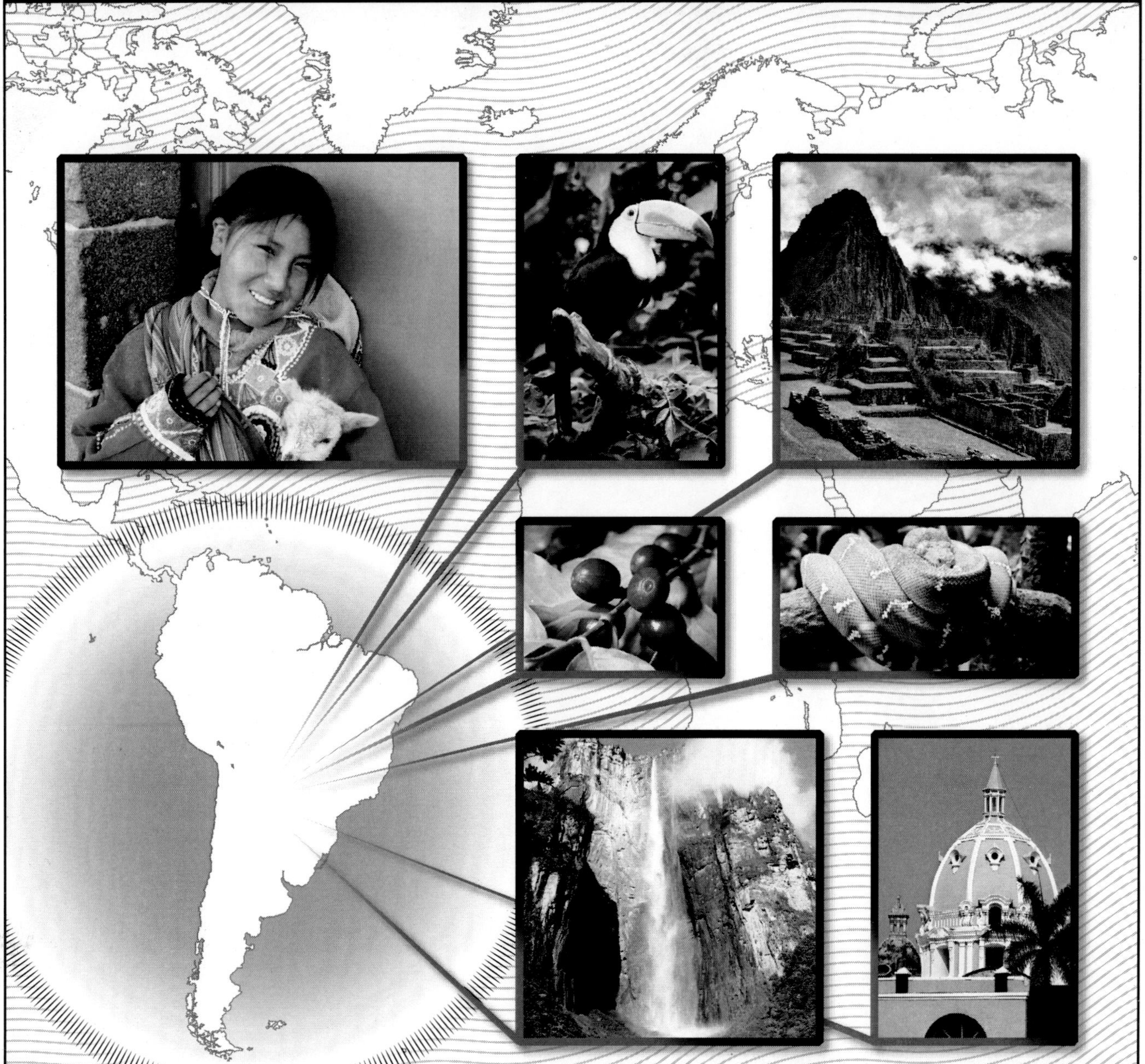

Exploring geography: South America
(Middle/Upper primary)

Published by Prim-Ed Publishing 2013 under licence from Evan-Moor® Educational Publishers

Copyright© 2010 Evan-Moor® Educational Publishers

This version copyright© Prim-Ed Publishing 2013

ISBN 978-1-84654-661-7
PR– 6366

Titles available in this series:
Beginning geography *(Lower/Middle primary)*
Exploring geography: Africa *(Middle/Upper primary)*
Exploring geography: Antarctica *(Middle/Upper primary)*
Exploring geography: Asia *(Middle/Upper primary)*
Exploring geography: Australia & Oceania *(Middle/Upper primary)*
Exploring geography: Europe *(Middle/Upper primary)*
Exploring geography: North America *(Middle/Upper primary)*
Exploring geography: South America *(Middle/Upper primary)*

This master may only be reproduced by the original purchaser for use with their class(es). The publisher prohibits the loaning or onselling of this master for the purposes of reproduction.

Copyright Notice

Blackline masters or copy masters are published and sold with a limited copyright. This copyright allows publishers to provide teachers and schools with a wide range of learning activities without copyright being breached. This limited copyright allows the purchaser to make sufficient copies for use within their own education institution. The copyright is not transferable, nor can it be onsold. Following these instructions is not essential but will ensure that you, as the purchaser, have evidence of legal ownership to the copyright if inspection occurs.

For your added protection in the case of copyright inspection, please complete the form below. Retain this form, the complete original document and the invoice or receipt as proof of purchase.

Name of Purchaser:
_____

Date of Purchase:
_____

Supplier:
_____

School Order# (if applicable):
_____

Signature of Purchaser:
_____

Internet websites
In some cases, websites or specific URLs may be recommended. While these are checked and rechecked at the time of publication, the publisher has no control over any subsequent changes which may be made to webpages. It is *strongly* recommended that the class teacher checks *all* URLs before allowing pupils to access them.

View all pages online   **Website:** www.prim-ed.com

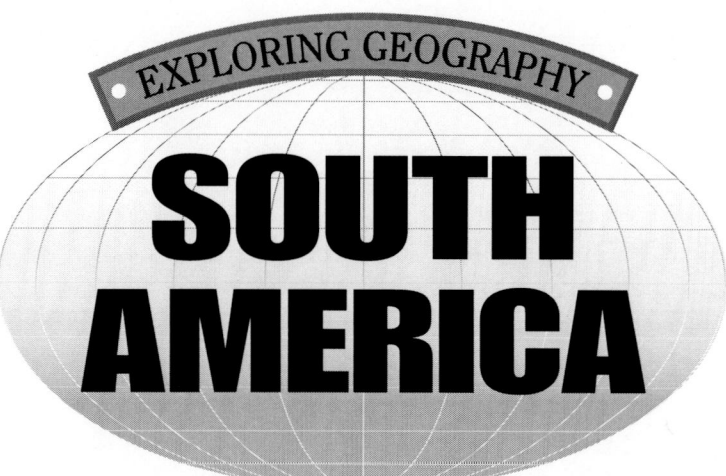

EXPLORING GEOGRAPHY
SOUTH AMERICA

CONTENTS

What's in this book 4

Section 1: South America in the world 5–16

Section 2: Political divisions of South America 17–42

Section 3: Physical features of South America 43–68

Section 4: Valuable resources of South America 69–90

Section 5: South American culture 91–110

Section 6: Assessment 111–114

Section 7: Note-takers 115–119

Answers 121–128

CURRICULUM LINKS

COUNTRY	SUBJECT	LEVEL	OBJECTIVES
England	Geography	KS 2	• locate the world's countries, using maps to focus on Europe and North and South America, concentrating on their environmental regions, key physical and human characteristics, countries and major cities • identify the position and significance of latitude, longitude, Equator, Northern Hemisphere, Southern Hemisphere, the Tropics of Cancer and Capricorn, Arctic and Antarctic Circle, and the Prime/Greenwich Meridian • understand geographical similarities and differences through the study of human and physical geography in a region of the United Kingdom, a region in a European country, and a region within North or South America • describe and understand key aspects of physical geography, including: climate zones, biomes and vegetation belts, rivers, mountains, volcanoes and earthquakes • describe and understand key aspects of human geography, including: types of settlement and land use, economic activity and the distribution of natural resources • use maps, atlases and globes to locate countries and describe features studied • use the eight points of a compass and symbols and key to build knowledge of the United Kingdom and the wider world

www.prim-ed.com Prim-Ed Publishing Exploring geography: South America 1

CURRICULUM LINKS

COUNTRY	SUBJECT	LEVEL	OBJECTIVES
Northern Ireland	The World Around Us	KS 1	• explore the interdependence of people and the environment • explore the effect of people on the natural environment over time • explore how place influences plant and animal life • explore features of the immediate world and comparisons between places • explore sources of energy in the world • study the life of a child in a contrasting location, including similarities and differences such as events and celebrations • compare the local area and a contrasting place; e.g. weather, landscape features
		KS 2	• explore the interdependence of people and the environment • explore the effect of people on the natural environment over time • explore how place influences the nature of life • explore features of, and variations in places, including physical, human, climatic, vegetation and animal life • know how we are interdependent with other parts of Europe and the wider world for some of our goods • compare places, such as location, size and resources • study weather in the local area compared to places that experience very different weather conditions • examine the effect of extreme weather conditions in the wider world, including the effect on places
Republic of Ireland	Geography	3rd/4th Class	• develop some awareness of the human and natural features of some places in other places in the world • establish and use cardinal compass points • develop familiarity with, and engage in practical use of maps • develop an understanding of and use some common map features and conventions • identify major geographical features and find places on the globe • develop some awareness of weather and climate in other parts of the world • develop some awareness of the types of environment which exist in other parts of the world
		5th/6th Class	• become familiar with the natural and human features of some places in other parts of the world • acquire an understanding of the relative location and size of major natural and human features • begin to develop an understanding of the names and relative location of some natural and human features of the world • develop some awareness of directions in wider environments • develop familiarity with, and engage in practical use of, maps • develop an understanding of and use common map features and conventions • recognise key lines of latitude and longitude on the globe • study some aspects of the environments and lives of people in one location in another part of the world • become familiar with the names and approximate location of a small number of major world physical features • become aware of the characteristics of some major climatic regions in different parts of the world

CURRICULUM LINKS

COUNTRY	SUBJECT	LEVEL	OBJECTIVES
Scotland	Social Studies	First	• explore climate zones around the world, and describe how climate affects living things • explore a natural environment different from their own, and discover how the physical features influence the variety of living things
		Second	• study a contrasting area outwith Britain and investigate the main features of weather and climate, discussing the impact on living things • interpret information from different maps, and locate key features within the UK, Europe or wider world
Wales	Geography	KS 2	• identify and locate places and environments using globes, atlases and maps • identify and describe natural and human features • identify similarities and differences to describe, compare and contrast places and environments • study living in other countries – contrasting localities outside the United Kingdom

NOTES

What's in this book

▶ **5 sections** of reproducible information and activity pages centred on five main topics: South America in the world, Political divisions, Physical features, Valuable resources and Culture.

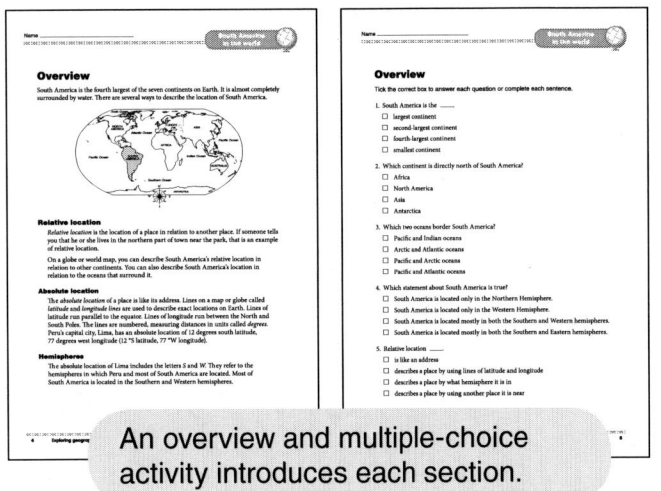

An overview and multiple-choice activity introduces each section.

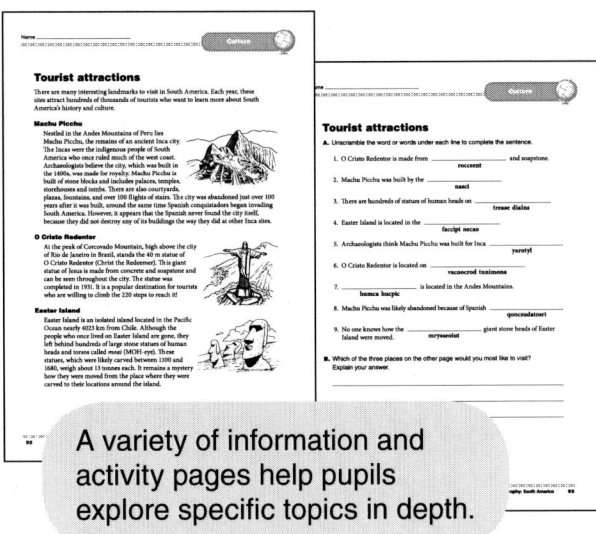

A variety of information and activity pages help pupils explore specific topics in depth.

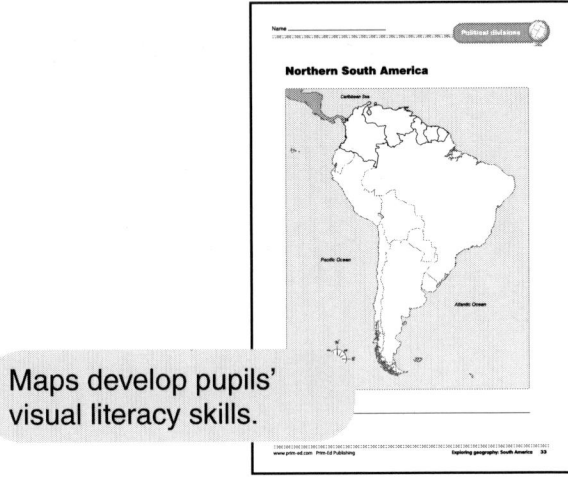

Maps develop pupils' visual literacy skills.

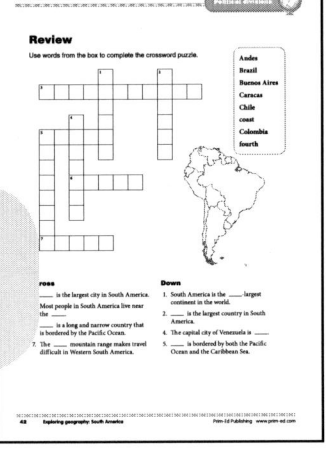

A crossword puzzle at the end of each section provides a fun review activity.

▶ **1 section** of assessment activities

▶ **1 section** of open-ended note-takers

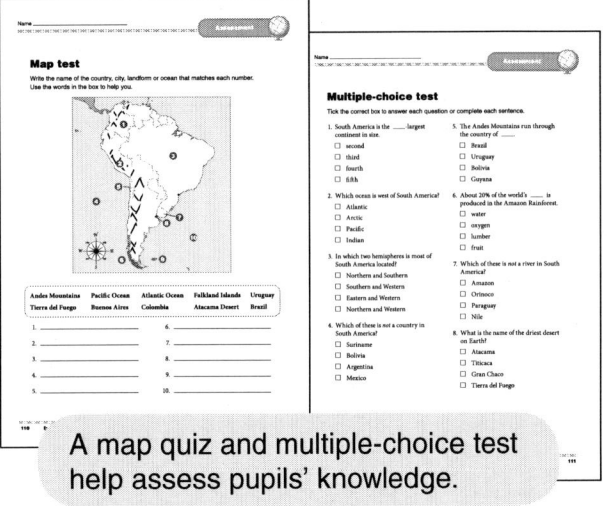

A map quiz and multiple-choice test help assess pupils' knowledge.

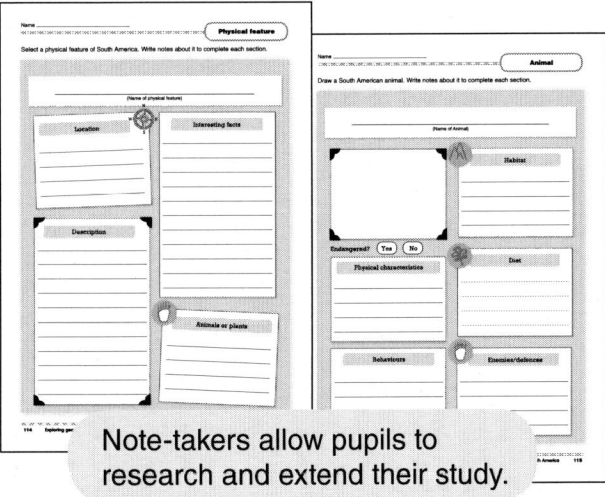

Note-takers allow pupils to research and extend their study.

South America in the world

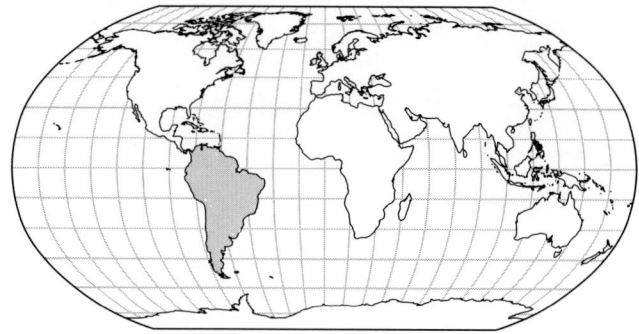

This section introduces pupils to the location of South America in the world. Pupils learn the difference between relative and absolute location, as well as the hemispheres in which South America lies. Pupils also practise using lines of latitude and longitude to find places on a map.

CONTENTS

Overview 6–7
South America's relative location 8–9
South America's hemispheres . 10–11
South America's absolute location 12–13
Using a projection map 14–15
Review 16

Name _____

South America in the world

Overview

South America is the fourth largest of the seven continents on Earth. It is almost completely surrounded by water. There are several ways to describe the location of South America.

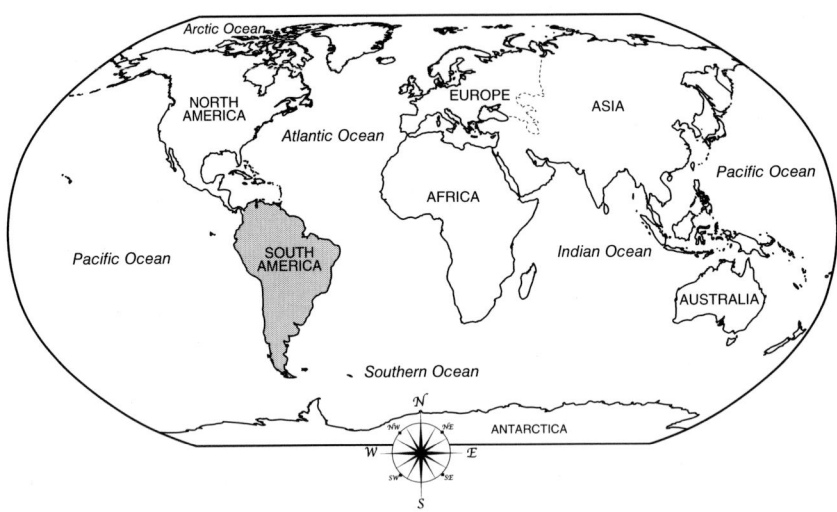

Relative location

Relative location is the location of a place in relation to another place. If someone tells you that he or she lives in the northern part of town near the park, that is an example of relative location.

On a globe or world map, you can describe South America's relative location in relation to other continents. You can also describe South America's location in relation to the oceans that surround it.

Absolute location

The *absolute location* of a place is like its address. Lines on a map or globe called *latitude* and *longitude lines* are used to describe exact locations on Earth. Lines of latitude run parallel to the equator. Lines of longitude run between the North and South Poles. The lines are numbered, measuring distances in units called *degrees*. Peru's capital city, Lima, has an absolute location of 12 degrees south latitude, 77 degrees west longitude (12 °S latitude, 77 °W longitude).

Hemispheres

The absolute location of Lima includes the letters *S* and *W*. They refer to the hemispheres in which Peru and most of South America are located. Most of South America is located in the Southern and Western hemispheres.

Name _____

South America in the world

Overview

Tick the correct box to answer each question or complete each sentence.

1. South America is the ____.
   ☐ largest continent
   ☐ second-largest continent
   ☐ fourth-largest continent
   ☐ smallest continent

2. Which continent is directly north of South America?
   ☐ Africa
   ☐ North America
   ☐ Asia
   ☐ Antarctica

3. Which two oceans border South America?
   ☐ Pacific and Indian oceans
   ☐ Arctic and Atlantic oceans
   ☐ Pacific and Arctic oceans
   ☐ Pacific and Atlantic oceans

4. Which statement about South America is true?
   ☐ South America is located only in the Northern Hemisphere.
   ☐ South America is located only in the Western Hemisphere.
   ☐ South America is located mostly in both the Southern and Western hemispheres.
   ☐ South America is located mostly in both the Southern and Eastern hemispheres.

5. Relative location ____.
   ☐ is like an address
   ☐ describes a place by using lines of latitude and longitude
   ☐ describes a place by what hemisphere it is in
   ☐ describes a place by using another place it is near

www.prim-ed.com   Prim-Ed Publishing   Exploring geography: South America   7

Name _____

South America in the world

South America's relative location

Relative location is the position of a place in relation to another place. How would you describe where South America is located in the world using relative location?

Look at the world map on page 9. One way to describe South America's relative location is to name the other continents that border it. For example; South America is west of Africa.

Another way to describe the relative location of South America is to name the oceans that surround the continent. For example; the Pacific Ocean is west of South America and the Atlantic Ocean is east of it.

A. Use the map on page 9 to complete the paragraph about the relative location of South America.

South America is the fourth-largest continent in the world. It is located west of the continent of _____. South America is also to the _____ of North America and north of the cold continent of _____. To the west is the huge _____ Ocean. The Atlantic Ocean is _____ of South America.

B. Follow the directions to colour the map on page 9.

1. Colour the continent north of South America orange.
2. Colour the continent east of South America yellow.
3. Circle in blue the name of the ocean that is east of South America.
4. Draw a penguin on the continent south of South America.

8   Exploring geography: South America   Prim-Ed Publishing   www.prim-ed.com

Name

South America's relative location

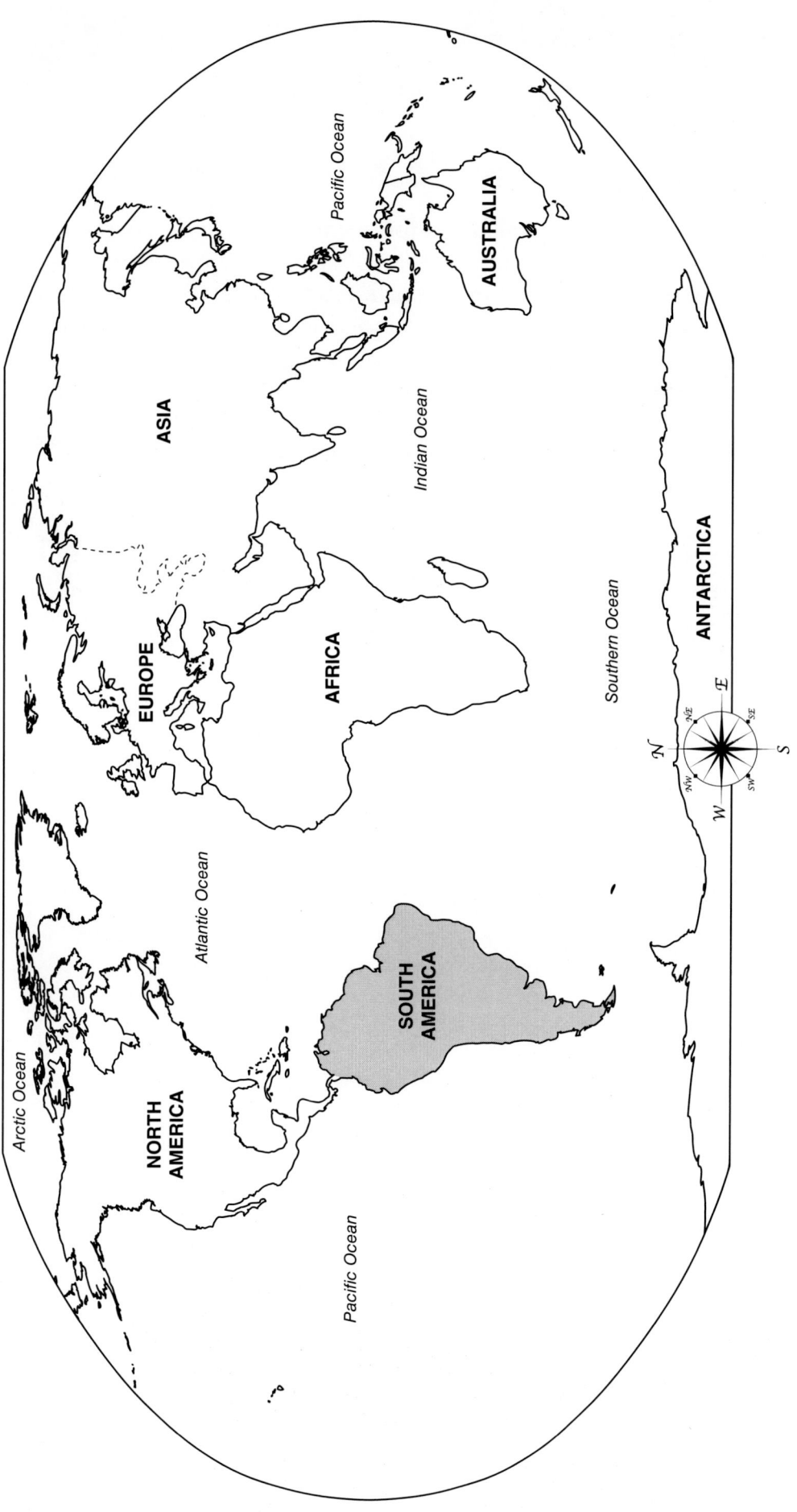

South America in the world

Name _____

South America in the world

South America's hemispheres

On a globe, Earth is divided into four hemispheres by a horizontal line called the *equator* and vertical lines that run from the North Pole to the South Pole. The hemispheres are the Northern, Southern, Western and Eastern. Most of South America is in the Southern Hemisphere because the majority of the continent is south of the equator. A small part of South America is located north of the equator, so that part is in the Northern Hemisphere. South America is also located in the Western Hemisphere.

Northern and Southern hemispheres

The globe shows an imaginary horizontal line that runs around the centre of the Earth. This line is called the *equator*. The equator divides the Earth into the Northern and Southern hemispheres.

Since most of South America is south of the equator, most of the continent is in the Southern Hemisphere.

Eastern and Western hemispheres

A globe also shows imaginary vertical lines that run from the North Pole to the South Pole, the southernmost point on Earth. One of these lines is called the *prime meridian*. This line, along with its twin line on the opposite side of the globe, creates the Eastern and Western hemispheres.

Since all of South America is west of the prime meridian, the continent is in the Western Hemisphere.

10 Exploring geography: South America   Prim-Ed Publishing   www.prim-ed.com

Name _____

South America in the world

South America's hemispheres

A. Write the letter of the definition that matches each term. Use the information and the pictures of the globes on page 10 to help you.

____ 1. South America
____ 2. continent
____ 3. globe
____ 4. equator
____ 5. Western Hemisphere
____ 6. hemisphere
____ 7. South Pole
____ 8. Southern Hemisphere
____ 9. prime meridian

a. an imaginary line that runs from the North Pole to the South Pole
b. half of the Earth
c. the continent that is mostly in both the Southern and Western hemispheres
d. the hemisphere that is west of the prime meridian
e. an imaginary line that divides Earth into the Northern and Southern hemispheres
f. any of the seven large landmasses of Earth
g. the southernmost point on Earth
h. a round model of the Earth
i. the hemisphere that is south of the equator

B. Label the parts of the globe. Use the letters next to the terms in the box.

A. Southern Hemisphere
B. South America
C. Western Hemisphere
D. Northern Hemisphere
E. equator
F. prime meridian

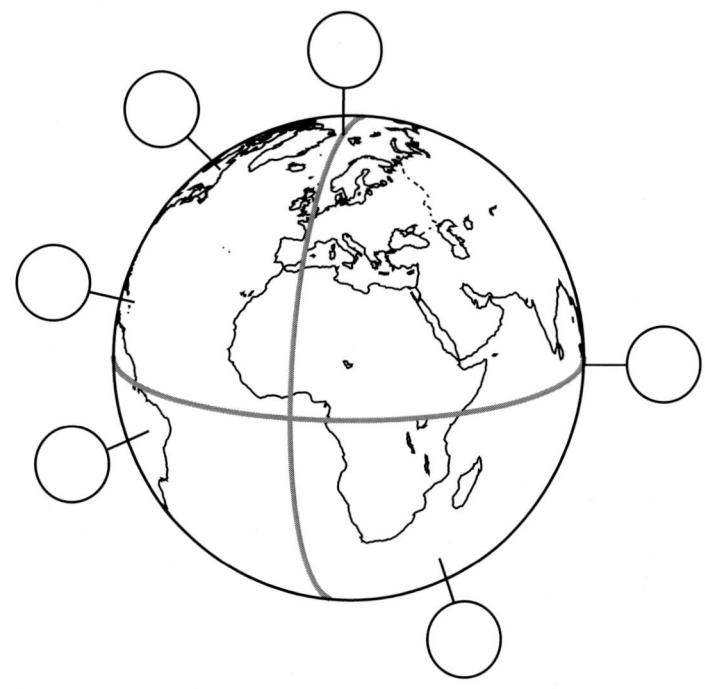

www.prim-ed.com   Prim-Ed Publishing   Exploring geography: South America   11

Name _____

South America in the world

South America's absolute location

Many globes contain lines that make it easier to find specific places on Earth. Lines of *latitude* measure the distance north and south of the equator. Lines of *longitude* measure the distance east and west of the prime meridian. You can use lines of latitude and longitude to find the absolute location of South America on a globe.

Latitude

The equator is found at the absolute location of 0 ° (zero degrees) latitude. Other lines of latitude run parallel to the equator and are labelled with an *N* or *S*, depending on whether they are north or south of the equator. Latitude lines are also called *parallels*.

On the picture of the globe, notice the lines of latitude. Look for the continent of South America. Since most of the continent is south of the equator, most of the latitude lines used to find the absolute location of places within South America are labelled in *degrees south*, or °S.

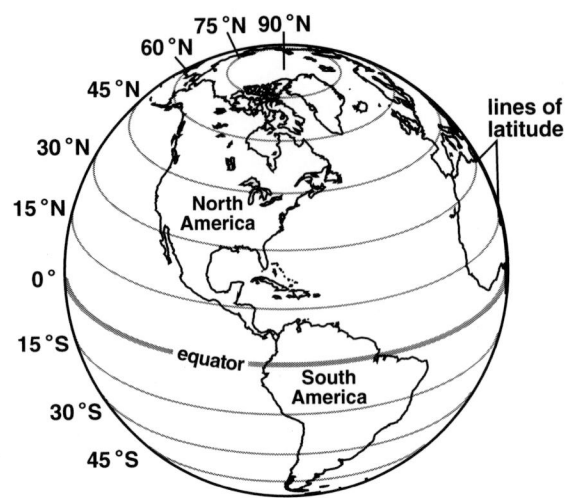

Lines of latitude (parallels)

Longitude

The prime meridian runs from the North Pole to the South Pole at 0 ° (zero degrees) longitude. Other lines of longitude run north and south, too, and are labelled with an *E* or *W*, depending on whether they are east or west of the prime meridian. Longitude lines are also called *meridians*.

On the picture of the globe, notice the lines of longitude. Look for the continent of South America. Since the continent is west of the prime meridian, all the longitude lines used to find the absolute location of places within South America are labelled in *degrees west*, or °W.

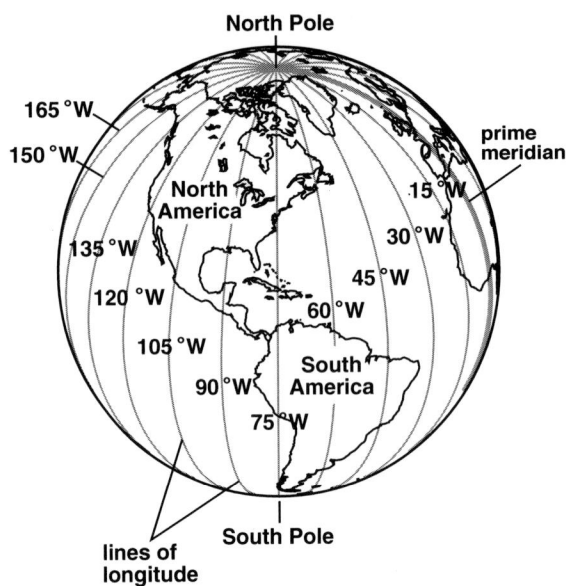

Lines of longitude (meridians)

12 Exploring geography: South America   Prim-Ed Publishing www.prim-ed.com

Name _____

South America in the world

South America's absolute location

To find the absolute location of a place, read the latitude line first, then the longitude line. For example, the latitude line 20 °S runs through the South American country of Paraguay. The longitude line 60 °W also runs through Paraguay. So the absolute location of Paraguay is 20 °S latitude, 60 °W longitude.

A. Circle the correct answer to each question. Use the information and the pictures of the globes on page 12 to help you.

1. Which line is at 0 degrees latitude?   equator   prime meridian

2. Which line runs north and south?   equator   prime meridian

3. Most of South America is in which direction from the equator?   north   south

4. Which longitude line runs through South America?   60 °E   60 °W

5. Where is the South Pole located?   90 °S   90 °N

6. Which lines run parallel to the equator?   latitude lines   longitude lines

7. How many degrees are between each line of latitude and longitude on the globes?   10 degrees   15 degrees

8. Which line of latitude is closer to the equator?   20 °N   30 °S

9. Which line of longitude is further west?   80 °W   70 °W

B. Using the information on page 12, explain why most places in South America have absolute locations that are labelled in degrees south and west.

_____

_____

www.prim-ed.com   Prim-Ed Publishing   Exploring geography: South America   13

Name _____

South America in the world

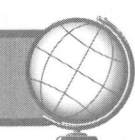

Using a projection map

How do you draw a picture of a round object, such as the Earth, on a flat piece of paper? In order to show all of Earth's continents and oceans in one view, mapmakers use a system called *projection*. Mapping the round Earth on a flat surface causes some areas to look bigger than they really are. For example, land near the poles gets stretched out when flattened. That's why Greenland and Antarctica look so big on some maps.

A projection map of the world shows all the lines of latitude and longitude on Earth. Study the projection map on page 15. Notice the lines of latitude and longitude. You can use these lines to find the absolute location of a specific place in South America. For example; the label *South America* is located at 10 °S latitude, 60 °W longitude.

A. Read each statement. Circle **yes** if it is true or **no** if it is false. Use the map on page 15 to help you.

1. South America is located on the prime meridian.   **Yes   No**

2. The equator runs through South America.   **Yes   No**

3. The southernmost part of South America is between the latitudes of 45 °S and 60 °S.   **Yes   No**

4. South America is the only continent west of the prime meridian.   **Yes   No**

5. South America shares some of the same south latitude lines with Africa.   **Yes   No**

6. South America shares some of the same east longitude lines with Europe.   **Yes   No**

7. The longitude line 60 °W runs through South America and North America.   **Yes   No**

8. The latitude line 30 °S runs through South America, Africa, and Australia.   **Yes   No**

B. How many continents can you find on the map that share the longitude line of 75 °W? Write their names.

_____

14   Exploring geography: South America   Prim-Ed Publishing   www.prim-ed.com

Name _____

South America in the world

Using a projection map

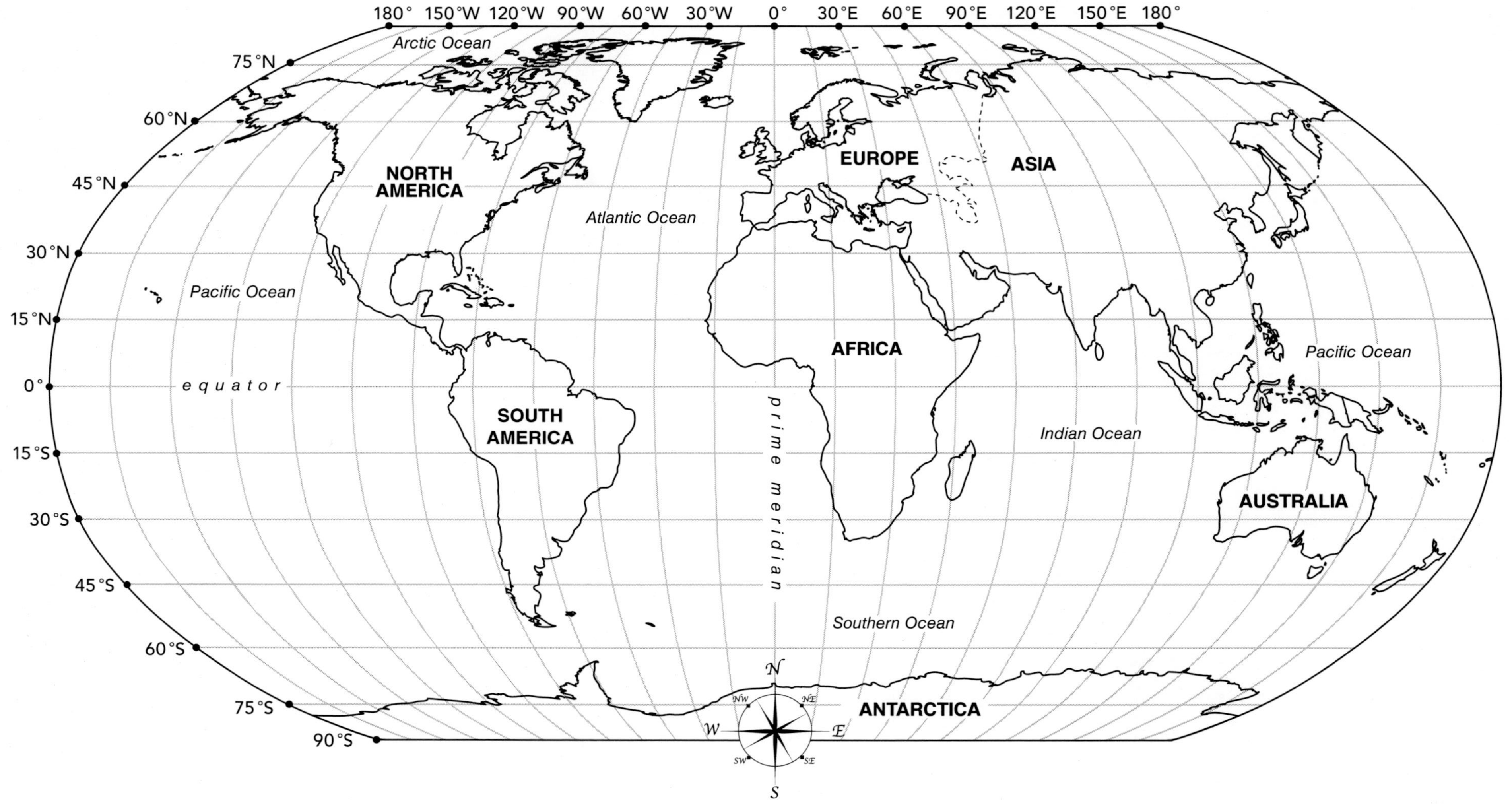

Name _____

South America in the world

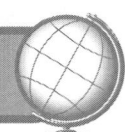

Review

Use words from the box to complete the crossword puzzle.

Word Box:
- Africa
- Atlantic
- equator
- fourth
- hemispheres
- Pacific
- projection
- relative

Across

2. If you go east of South America, you will find the ____ Ocean.
3. South America is part of the Southern and Western ____.
6. The continent of ____ is east of South America.
8. A ____ map shows the round Earth on a flat surface.

Down

1. The Atlantic and ____ oceans border South America.
4. The ____ location is the position of a place in relation to another place.
5. The ____ is the imaginary line that divides Earth into Northern and Southern hemispheres.
7. South America is the ____-largest continent in the world.

Political divisions of South America

This section introduces pupils to the three regions and 12 countries of South America. Pupils learn how the regions differ in size and population, and study data about the largest countries and cities within each region. Pupils also learn about the capital cities of South America.

CONTENTS

Overview.................................. 18–19
Population of South America.. 20–21
Countries of South America.... 22–23
Largest countries by area 24–25
Largest countries by population 26–27
Western South America.......... 28–29
Population of Western South America 30–31
Northern South America......... 32–33
Population of Northern South America 34–35
Eastern South America........... 36–37
Population of Eastern South America 38–39
Capital cities of South America 40–41
Review 42

Name _____

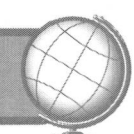

Political divisions

Overview

South America is the fourth-largest continent in size and the fifth-largest in population.

- South America covers about 12% of the world's landmass.
- South America has about 6% of the world's people—385 million.

The three regions

The 12 countries in South America can be divided into three regions.

Region	Number of countries	Fast facts
Western	4	includes the third-largest country in size—Peru
Northern	4	includes the second most populated country—Colombia
Eastern	4	includes the largest country in size and population—Brazil

Where people live

Brazil is by far the largest South American country in size, and it is also the most heavily populated. In fact, Brazil has about the same number of people as the 11 other countries of South America combined.

The largest areas of population in South America are near the coast, with the middle of the continent being much less populated. Most people in South America live in big cities. Many have moved from rural areas to cities in search of better jobs. With over 11 million people living in the city and surrounding areas, Buenos Aires, Argentina, is the largest city in South America. São Paulo, Brazil, is nearly as big. Other large cities include Lima, Peru; Bogotá, Colombia; and Rio de Janeiro, Brazil.

Name _____

Political divisions

Overview

Tick the correct box to answer each question or complete each sentence.

1. South America is the ____-largest continent in population.
   ☐ second
   ☐ third
   ☐ fourth
   ☐ fifth

2. There are ____ countries in South America.
   ☐ 3
   ☐ 12
   ☐ 14
   ☐ 50

3. ____ is the largest country in South America.
   ☐ Brazil
   ☐ Argentina
   ☐ Peru
   ☐ Colombia

4. Most people in South America live ____.
   ☐ in the country
   ☐ in the desert
   ☐ near the coast
   ☐ in São Paulo

5. Which of these is *not* one of the largest cities in South America?
   ☐ São Paulo
   ☐ Lima
   ☐ Rio de Janeiro
   ☐ Cairo

Population of South America

A *population census* is a survey by a national government to gather information about the number of people who live in that country. Population censuses have been conducted since ancient times. The earliest known population counts were made by the Chinese and Egyptians. Today, most countries conduct an official census every 10 years. In addition, experts look at the data from the past to predict what the population will be in the future.

Between 1950 and 2010, the world population nearly tripled to almost 7 billion. The population of South America is growing even faster than that of the world. In 1950, there were about 112 million people living in South America. By 2010, that number was nearly four times higher at 395 million. By 2050, South America's population is expected to increase by another 85 million.

A. Colour each bar on the graph a different colour. Then use the information above to write a caption about the graph. Include at least two interesting facts in the caption.

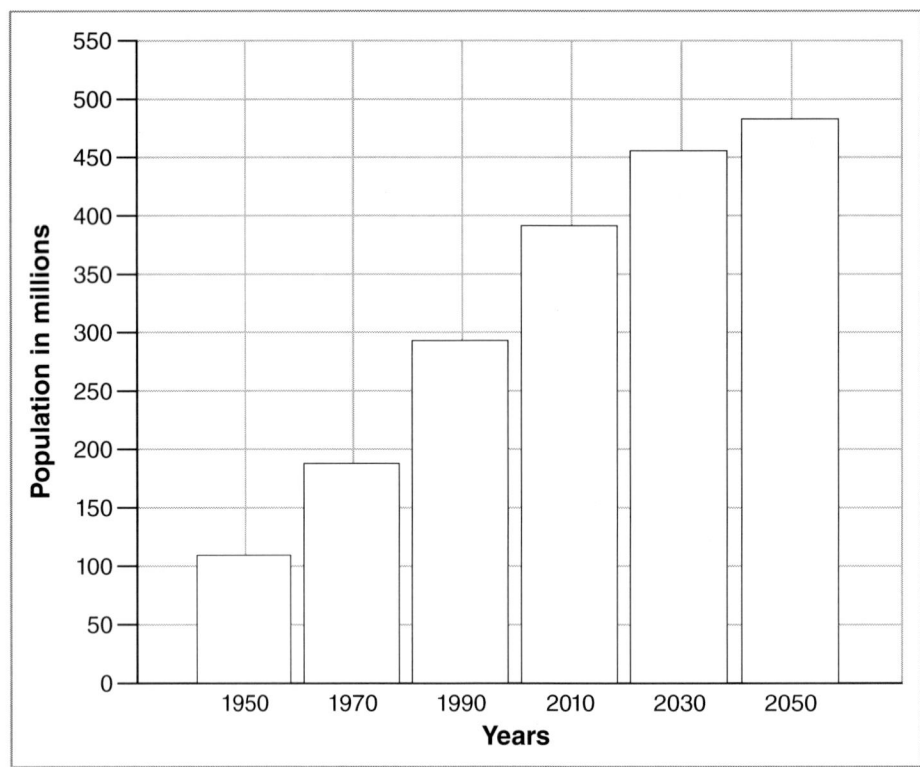

South America's population: 1950–2050

Source: United Nations Database

Name _____

Political divisions

Population of South America

B. Circle the answer that completes each sentence. Use the graph and information on page 20 to help you.

1. The population of the world has nearly ___ since 1950.

   doubled   **tripled**   **quadrupled**

2. The population of South America is growing ___ the world population.

   the same as   **faster than**   **slower than**

3. In 1950, there were about ___ million people living in South America.

   112   **191**   **393**

4. In 1990, there were nearly ___ million people living in South America.

   200   **300**   **400**

5. By 2030, there will be about ___ million people living in South America.

   458   **483**   **393**

6. There were about 191 million people living in South America in ___.

   1950   **1970**   **2010**

7. There will be about 483 million people living in South America by ___.

   2030   **2050**   **2070**

C. Write two new questions based on the information in the graph. Then answer the questions you wrote.

1. _____

   _____

2. _____

   _____

Name _____

Political divisions

Countries of South America

South America is made up of 12 countries. Brazil is by far the largest in size, and Suriname is the smallest. In addition to the 12 independent countries, South America also has two *dependencies,* or territories. French Guiana in Northern South America is a dependency of France. The Falkland Islands, located just east of the southern tip of South America, are a dependency of the United Kingdom.

A. Look at the chart below. Find the countries on the map on page 23. Then use the colour key below the map to colour the regions.

Region	Countries	Dependencies
Western	Bolivia, Chile, Ecuador, Peru	none
Northern	Colombia, Guyana, Suriname, Venezuela	French Guiana
Eastern	Argentina, Brazil, Paraguay, Uruguay	Falkland Islands

B. Read each statement. Circle **yes** if it is true or **no** if it is false. Use the map on page 23 and the information above to help you.

1. Suriname is the largest country in South America.   Yes   No

2. There are two dependencies in South America.   Yes   No

3. Venezuela is part of the Western region.   Yes   No

4. There are no dependencies in the Eastern region.   Yes   No

5. Peru is west of Brazil.   Yes   No

6. Bolivia and Paraguay do not border an ocean.   Yes   No

7. The Pacific Ocean is east of Chile.   Yes   No

8. Brazil borders every South American country except Ecuador and Chile.   Yes   No

9. Bolivia is south of Argentina.   Yes   No

22 Exploring geography: South America   Prim-Ed Publishing www.prim-ed.com

Name _____

Political divisions

Countries of South America

Colour key

Western region: Yellow   **Northern region:** Green   **Eastern region:** Red

Name _____

Political divisions

Largest countries by area

With the exceptions of Brazil and Argentina, most South American countries are rather small compared to many other countries in the world.

Rank in size	Country	Square kilometres
1	Brazil	8 514 873
2	Argentina	2 780 400
3	Peru	1 285 214
4	Colombia	1 138 914
5	Bolivia	1 098 580

A. Write three true statements that can be made about South America's five largest countries, using information in the chart.

1. _____

_____

2. _____

_____

3. _____

_____

B. On the map on page 25, five countries are numbered. The numbers indicate the rank of each country according to size. Colour each country a different colour. Then complete the map key by writing the country names in order from largest to smallest. Write the colour you used for each country.

24 Exploring geography: South America   Prim-Ed Publishing www.prim-ed.com

Name _____

Political divisions

Largest countries by area

MAP KEY

Country　　　　　　　　　　　　Colour

1. _____　　_____

2. _____　　_____

3. _____　　_____

4. _____　　_____

5. _____　　_____

Largest countries by population

Compared to most other continents, South America is sparsely populated. Only about 6% of the world's population lives in South America. Brazil is by far the most populated country with nearly 200 million people. Colombia, the second most populated country, has only about a quarter the population of Brazil.

	Country	Population
1	Brazil	198 739 269
2	Colombia	43 677 372
3	Argentina	40 913 584
4	Peru	29 546 963
5	Venezuela	26 814 843

A. Use the chart above to make a bar graph showing how many people live in each of the five most populated countries in South America. Round off the numbers to the nearest million. Then colour each bar a different colour.

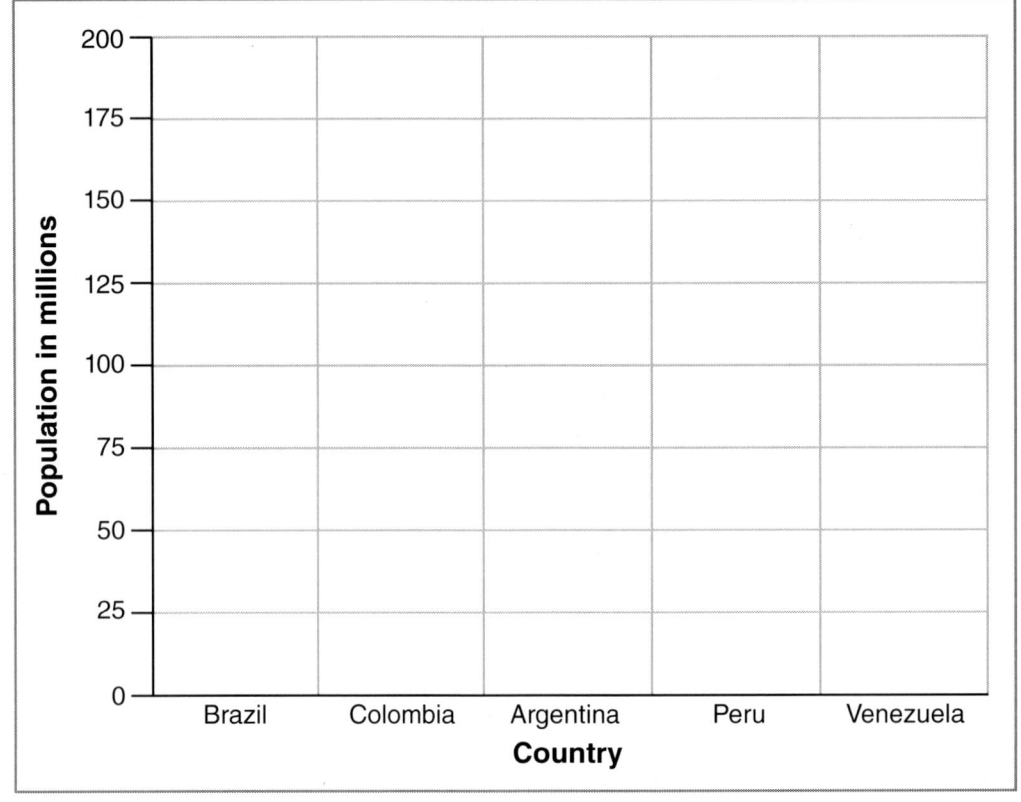

Name _____

Political divisions

Largest countries by population

B. Fill in the blanks to complete each sentence. Use the information on page 26 to help you.

1. Of the world's population, only about _____ % lives in South America.

2. _____ is the second most populated country in South America.

3. _____ and _____ each have more than 40 million people, but fewer than 50 million.

4. _____ has a higher population than Venezuela, but a lower population than Argentina.

5. The country of _____ is the fifth most populated country in South America.

6. _____ is the largest country in population.

C. Write three true statements about the most populated countries of South America, using the information on page 26.

1. _____
   _____

2. _____
   _____

3. _____
   _____

www.prim-ed.com Prim-Ed Publishing   Exploring geography: South America 27

Name _____

Political divisions

Western South America

Four countries make up the western region of South America. They are Bolivia, Chile, Ecuador and Peru. All of these countries are dominated by the Andes Mountains, which run along the west coast from north to south.

The largest country in Western South America is Peru. Peru is about 1 285 000 square kilometres in size, or about two-thirds the size of Mexico. Chile, though not the largest, is by far the longest. It stretches 4345 km from the southern border of Peru all the way to the southern tip of the continent, where it is only 644 km from Antarctica. In addition to being long, Chile is also very narrow, averaging only about 177 km across.

Bolivia is the only country in this region that does not border the Pacific Ocean. The Andes run through the western third of Bolivia. The smallest and most northern country of the region is Ecuador.

A. Use the information above to label each of the four countries in the Western region on the map on page 29. Colour each country a different colour, then write a caption about the map.

B. Read each statement. Circle **yes** if it is true or **no** if it is false. Use the information on this page and the map on page 29 to help you.

1. The Andes Mountains run from north to south.   Yes   No

2. Bolivia is the largest country in Western South America.   Yes   No

3. Chile is 4345 km long.   Yes   No

4. The Pacific Ocean borders all of the countries in the Western region.   Yes   No

5. Ecuador is the second-smallest country in Western South America.   Yes   No

6. Bolivia borders Chile to the north-east.   Yes   No

7. Ecuador is south of Peru.   Yes   No

8. Bolivia is a long and narrow country.   Yes   No

Name _____

Political divisions

Western South America

_____

_____

www.prim-ed.com Prim-Ed Publishing

Exploring geography: South America **29**

Name _____

Political divisions

Population of Western South America

With nearly 30 million people, Peru is the most populated of the four countries of Western South America. However, this is a small population when compared to other countries of a similar size in the world. For example, Mexico, which is only one-third larger than Peru, has more than three times as many people.

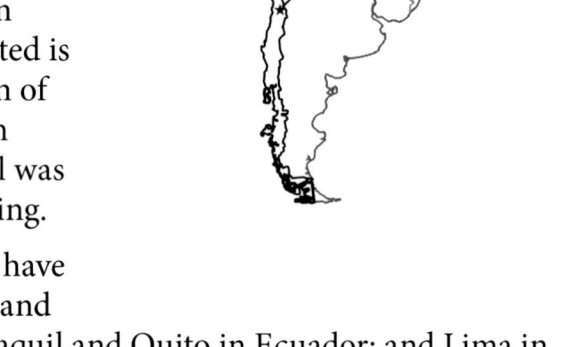

The reason that Peru and the other countries in Western South America are so sparsely populated is that the Andes Mountains cover a large portion of the land. Few people choose to live in the harsh mountain climate. In addition, before air travel was possible, crossing the Andes was very challenging.

Only six cities in this region of South America have populations over one million. They are La Paz and Santa Cruz in Bolivia; Santiago in Chile; Guayaquil and Quito in Ecuador; and Lima in Peru.

A. Use the chart to write the six largest cities in Western South America in order by population. The largest city should be **1**.

Country	Population	Cities with populations over 1 million
Bolivia	9 775 246	• La Paz (population: 1 517 000) • Santa Cruz (population: 1 595 000)
Chile	16 601 707	• Santiago (population: 5 278 000)
Ecuador	14 573 100	• Guayaquil (population: 2 196 000) • Quito (population: 1 648 100)
Peru	29 546 963	• Lima (population: 7 606 000)

1. _____   4. _____

2. _____   5. _____

3. _____   6. _____

30   Exploring geography: South America   Prim-Ed Publishing   www.prim-ed.com

Name _____

Political divisions

Population of Western South America

B. Fill in the blanks with the correct words to complete the paragraph. Use the information on page 30 to help you.

Of the four countries of Western South America, _____ is the most populated. The countries in this region are sparsely populated because the _____ mountain range covers much of the land. Six _____ in Western South America have populations over one million. The largest city is _____, which is located in Peru.

C. Write the letter of the clue that matches each country or city. Use the chart on page 30 to help you.

____ 1. Chile
____ 2. Guayaquil
____ 3. Lima
____ 4. Peru
____ 5. La Paz
____ 6. Bolivia
____ 7. Quito
____ 8. Santa Cruz
____ 9. Ecuador
____ 10. Santiago

a. the country with the smallest population in Western South America
b. the largest city in Chile
c. the largest city in Ecuador
d. a city with a population of 1 595 000
e. the second most populated country in the region
f. the largest city in Western South America
g. a city in Ecuador with fewer than 2 million people
h. the most populated country in the region
i. the third most populated country in Western South America
j. the second-largest city in Bolivia

www.prim-ed.com   Prim-Ed Publishing   Exploring geography: South America   31

Name _____

Political divisions

Northern South America

Northern South America includes the countries of Colombia, Guyana, Suriname and Venezuela, as well as the dependency of French Guiana. Colombia is the largest of these countries. It is bordered on the west by the Pacific Ocean and on the north by the Caribbean Sea. The Central American country of Panama borders Colombia to the north-west.

Venezuela lies east of Colombia and is nearly as large. To the east of Venezuela is Guyana. Guyana, which means 'land of many flowing waters', was given that name because of the many rivers that flow through the country. To the east of Guyana is Suriname, the smallest of the South American countries. Almost all of Suriname is covered in rainforest. Even smaller than Suriname is the dependency of French Guiana, which is the furthest east.

A. Use the information above to label each of the four countries and the dependency in the northern region on the map on page 33. Colour each place a different colour, then write a caption about the map.

B. Fill in the blanks to answer each question. Use the information on this page and the map on page 33 to help you.

1. How many countries are in Northern South America? _____

2. Which country is the second largest in area? _____

3. Which country is bordered by two different bodies of water? _____

4. Which country is the smallest in the northern region? _____

5. What is the name of the only dependency in Northern South America? _____

6. Which country is bordered by both Venezuela and Suriname? _____

7. Why was Guyana given its name?

_____

Name _____

Political divisions

Northern South America

Population of Northern South America

With more than 43 million people, Colombia is the most populated country in Northern South America. The next most populated country, Venezuela, has about half the population of Colombia. Guyana and Suriname both have small populations. The combined population of both countries is only a little more than Dublin, the capital city of Ireland.

Four of the seven largest cities in this region are located in Colombia. Bogotá is the largest, with more than 6 million people. The other Colombian cities with populations over 1 million are Cali, Medellín and Barranquilla. The cities of Maracaibo, Caracas and Valencia, all in Venezuela, also have populations over 1 million.

The chart below shows the populations of the four countries of Northern South America, as well as interesting facts about each country's population.

Country	Population	Interesting population facts
Colombia	43 677 372	• Most of the people live on the west side of the country in or near the capital city of Bogotá. • Most of the population is Mestizo (a mix of South American Indian and European ancestry).
Venezuela	26 814 843	• Nearly 90% of the population lives in cities. • About 50% of the population is under 25 years old.
Guyana	752 940	• Most of the people are descendants of slaves from Africa or indentured servants from India who were brought to the country to work on sugar cane plantations. • More than 90% of the population lives along the coast.
Suriname	481 267	• Nearly 15% of the population of Suriname are Maroons, people whose ancestors escaped from slavery. • Suriname's population is ranked 170 of the 267 nations of the world.

Name _____

Political divisions

Population of Northern South America

Read each clue below. Write the correct word on the numbered lines. Then use the numbers to crack the code!

1. ____ is the second most populated country in Northern South America.

   $\overline{5}$ $\overline{22}$ $\overline{13}$ $\overline{22}$ $\overline{1}$ $\overline{6}$ $\overline{22}$ $\overline{15}$ $\overline{26}$

2. ____ is the largest city and capital of Colombia.

   $\overline{25}$ $\overline{12}$ $\overline{20}$ $\overline{12}$ $\overline{7}$ $\overline{26}$

3. ____ is the most populated country in Northern South America.

   $\overline{24}$ $\overline{12}$ $\overline{15}$ $\overline{12}$ $\overline{14}$ $\overline{25}$ $\overline{18}$ $\overline{26}$

4. More than 90% of the population of ____ lives along the coast.

   $\overline{20}$ $\overline{6}$ $\overline{2}$ $\overline{26}$ $\overline{13}$ $\overline{26}$

5. ____ is one of the largest cities in Venezuela.

   $\overline{14}$ $\overline{26}$ $\overline{9}$ $\overline{26}$ $\overline{24}$ $\overline{26}$ $\overline{18}$ $\overline{25}$ $\overline{12}$

6. ____ people are of mixed South American Indian and European ancestry.

   $\overline{14}$ $\overline{22}$ $\overline{8}$ $\overline{7}$ $\overline{18}$ $\overline{1}$ $\overline{12}$

7. Suriname is ____ 170 in the world in population.

   $\overline{9}$ $\overline{26}$ $\overline{13}$ $\overline{10}$ $\overline{22}$ $\overline{23}$

Crack the code!

The world's largest supply of ____ comes from Colombia.

$\overline{22}$ $\overline{14}$ $\overline{22}$ $\overline{9}$ $\overline{26}$ $\overline{15}$ $\overline{23}$ $\overline{8}$

www.prim-ed.com   Prim-Ed Publishing   Exploring geography: South America

Name _____

Political divisions

Eastern South America

Eastern South America is the largest of the three regions on the continent. It includes the countries of Argentina, Brazil, Paraguay and Uruguay, as well as the Falkland Islands, which are a dependency of the United Kingdom. Brazil covers almost half the total land area in South America and is the fifth-largest country in the world. Argentina is about one-third the size of Brazil and stretches to the southern tip of South America.

Paraguay is a landlocked country that is sandwiched between Brazil and Argentina. It is dependent on its many rivers as links to the Atlantic Ocean. Uruguay is the smallest country in this region and the second-smallest country in South America. The Falkland Islands lie in the Atlantic Ocean, just east of the southern tip of the continent.

A. Use the information above to label each of the four countries and the dependency in Eastern South America on the map on page 37. Colour each place a different colour. Then write a caption about the map.

B. Complete each sentence by unscrambling the word or words under the line. Use the information above and the map on page 37 to help you.

Some of the answers will need to start with capital letters.

1. The Falkland Islands are a _____ of Great Britain.
   ecynnddeep

2. _____ is the fifth-largest country in the world.
   ziblar

3. _____ is about one-third the size of Brazil.
   tearnaing

4. The only landlocked country in this region is _____.
   auyaprag

5. _____ is bordered to the north-east by Brazil.
   raguuyu

6. The country of _____ stretches to the tip of the continent.
   gtianeran

7. Brazil is bordered to the east by the _____.
   tiltanac nacoe

8. Argentina is _____ of the Falkland Islands.
   swte

Name _____

Political divisions

Eastern South America

Caribbean Sea

Pacific Ocean

Atlantic Ocean

N, NE, E, SE, S, SW, W, NW

Population of Eastern South America

Most of the people in South America live in Eastern South America, especially in the large cities of Brazil and Argentina. There are 18 cities in this region that have populations of over 1 million. The two most populated cities are Buenos Aires, Argentina and São Paulo, Brazil. Each of these cities has more than 11 million people.

	City	Country	Population
1	Buenos Aires	Argentina	11 655 000
2	São Paulo	Brazil	11 038 000
3	Rio de Janeiro	Brazil	6 093 000
4	Salvador da Bahia	Brazil	2 998 000
5	Fortaleza	Brazil	2 506 000
6	Belo Horizonte	Brazil	2 453 000
7	Brasília	Brazil	2 089 000
8	Curitiba	Brazil	1 851 000
9	Manaus	Brazil	1 739 000
10	Recife	Brazil	1 561 000
11	Belém	Brazil	1 409 000
12	Pôrto Alegre	Brazil	1 355 000
13	Montevideo	Uruguay	1 326 000
14	Córdoba	Argentina	1 310 000
15	Guarulhos	Brazil	1 283 000
16	Goiânia	Brazil	1 282 000
17	Rosario	Argentina	1 160 000
18	Campinas	Brazil	1 059 000

Name _____

Political divisions

Population of Eastern South America

A. Unscramble the names of the cities in Eastern South America. Then write the names of the countries they are located in. Use the information and chart on page 38 to help you.

1. libsraai: _____ _____
                        city   country

2. meleb: _____ _____
                        city   country

3. nobuse risae: _____ _____
                        city   country

4. osrario: _____ _____
                        city   country

B. Circle the correct answer for each clue. Use the chart on page 38 to help you.

1.	Uruguay's most populated city	**Pôrto Alegre**	**Montevideo**
2.	the fifth most populated city in the region	**Fortaleza**	**Brasília**
3.	the number of cities with over 3 million people	**five**	**three**
4.	the country in which Fortaleza is located	**Brazil**	**Argentina**
5.	a city in Argentina	**Curitiba**	**Córdoba**
6.	the population of Rosario	**1 160 000**	**1 225 000**
7.	a city with just over 2 million people	**Brasília**	**Manaus**
8.	the largest city in Brazil	**Buenos Aires**	**São Paulo**
9.	a city in Brazil that is less populated than Goiânia	**Guarulhos**	**Campinas**
10.	a city with just over 2.5 million people	**Recife**	**Fortaleza**

Name _____

Political divisions

Capital cities of South America

Every country in South America has a capital city, which is the central location of the country's government. The capital city contains government buildings where leaders meet and laws are made. Often the president, prime minister, or other leaders of the country live in the capital city.

In many South American countries, such as Paraguay and Peru, the capital city is also the most populated city in the country. However, in a few countries, such as Brazil and Ecuador, the capital is *not* the largest city.

Country	Capital city	Country	Capital city
Argentina	Buenos Aires*	Guyana	Georgetown*
Bolivia	La Paz—administrative; Sucre—constitutional	Paraguay	Asunción*
Brazil	Brasília	Peru	Lima*
Chile	Santiago*	Suriname	Paramaribo*
Colombia	Bogotá*	Uruguay	Montevideo*
Ecuador	Quito	Venezuela	Caracas*

*Also the most populated city in the country

Find each country listed above on the map on page 41. Use the chart to match the number on the map to the correct capital city. Write the name of the city next to the correct number below. (For Bolivia, write the name of the administrative capital.) Then colour the countries whose capital cities are also the most populated cities.

1. _____
2. _____
3. _____
4. _____
5. _____
6. _____
7. _____
8. _____
9. _____
10. _____
11. _____
12. _____

40 Exploring geography: South America Prim-Ed Publishing www.prim-ed.com

Name _____

Political divisions

Capital cities of South America

Name _____

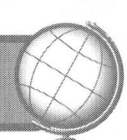

Political divisions

Review

Use words from the box to complete the crossword puzzle.

Andes
Brazil
Buenos Aires
Caracas
Chile
coast
Colombia
fourth

Across

3. ____ is the largest city in South America.
5. Most people in South America live near the ____.
6. ____ is a long and narrow country that is bordered by the Pacific Ocean.
7. The ____ mountain range makes travel difficult in Western South America.

Down

1. South America is the ____-largest continent in the world.
2. ____ is the largest country in South America.
4. The capital city of Venezuela is ____.
5. ____ is bordered by both the Pacific Ocean and the Caribbean Sea.

42   Exploring geography: South America   Prim-Ed Publishing   www.prim-ed.com

SECTION 3

Physical features of South America

In this section, pupils learn about the landforms and bodies of water of South America. Pupils discover that South America is home to some of the most interesting landforms on Earth, including the Andes Mountains and the Amazon Rainforest. They learn about the vast plains and highlands of South America, as well as one of its deserts. Pupils also become familiar with the major lakes and rivers of South America.

CONTENTS

Overview.................................. 44–45	Tierra del Fuego 58–59
South America's landscape 46–47	South America's bodies of water 60–61
Andes Mountains.................... 48–49	Amazon River 62–63
Highlands of South America.... 50–51	Lake Titicaca 64–65
Plains of South America 52–53	Angel Falls.................................... 66
Amazon Rainforest 54–55	Review.. 67
Atacama Desert...................... 56–57	

Name _____

Physical features

Overview

South America is a large continent that is almost completely surrounded by water. It is connected to North America by only a thin strip of land in the Central American country of Panama. South America has many interesting natural features.

Landforms

South America has three main types of physical features: mountains, highlands and lowlands.

The Andes mountain system is the longest mountain chain in the world. It stretches 8851 km down almost the entire western coast of South America. The tallest mountain in the Andes is Mount Aconcagua.

Andes Mountains

The Guiana Highlands and the Brazilian Highlands have rounded hills and lower, often flat-topped mountains called *tepuis*. Most of this area is sparsely populated. Further south is an area of highlands called Patagonia.

The lowlands separate the highlands from one another. The lowlands run from the Llanos Plains in the north and then south through the largest rainforest in the world, the Amazon. The lowlands of the Gran Chaco and the Pampas are south of the Amazon.

Bodies of water

South America is bordered by the Pacific Ocean on the west and the Atlantic Ocean on the east. The Caribbean Sea is located to the north of the continent.

South America contains the second-longest river in the world, the Amazon River, which flows through the rainforest in Brazil.

Amazon River

One of the world's highest lakes, Lake Titicaca, is also located in South America. Lake Titicaca is 3810 m above sea level in the Andes Mountains.

Beautiful waterfalls can also be found in South America, including Angel Falls, the tallest waterfall in the world.

Name _____

Physical features

Overview

Tick the correct box to answer each question or complete each sentence.

1. Which of these is *not* a major physical feature of South America?
   ☐ Patagonian Plateau
   ☐ Brazilian Highlands
   ☐ Andes Mountains
   ☐ Southern Tundra

2. Which of these is the tallest mountain in the Andes mountain system?
   ☐ Mount Aconcagua
   ☐ Mount Titicaca
   ☐ Mount Guiana
   ☐ Mount Tepuis

3. Which of these is *not* an area of lowlands?
   ☐ Amazon Rainforest
   ☐ Llanos Plains
   ☐ Pampas
   ☐ Patagonia

4. The Amazon River is the ____-longest river in the world.
   ☐ second
   ☐ third
   ☐ fourth
   ☐ fifth

5. Which statement about South America is *not* true?
   ☐ South America is almost completely surrounded by water.
   ☐ South America has one of the highest lakes in the world.
   ☐ South America is bordered only by the Atlantic Ocean and Caribbean Sea.
   ☐ South America has many rivers.

Name _____

Physical features

South America's landscape

South America has a diverse landscape. The west is dominated by the Andes Mountains, which stretch almost the entire length of the continent. There are three large areas of highlands on the eastern side of the continent—the Guiana Highlands, the Brazilian Highlands and Patagonia. The highlands are separated by lowland areas. The largest lowlands area is the Amazon Basin, a hot, wet rainforest. Other lowland areas are grassy or dry plains. At the far south, the land is covered in ice and snow.

A. Study the physical map of South America on page 47. Use the information and the map to write the correct answers.

1. Which landform runs along the entire west coast? _____

2. What is the name of the desert on the west coast? _____

3. What is the name of the mountain peak shown on the map? _____

4. Which highlands are furthest east? _____

5. Which highlands are in the north? _____

6. What is the name of the island group just east of the southern tip of South America? _____

7. Which highlands are furthest south? _____

8. Is the Amazon Basin in the northern or southern part of the continent? _____

B. Colour the map according to the directions below.

1. Colour the Andes Mountains brown.

2. Colour the Atacama Desert yellow.

3. Circle Patagonia and the Guiana and Brazilian highlands in orange.

4. Circle the Amazon Basin in green.

Name _____

Physical features

South America's landscape

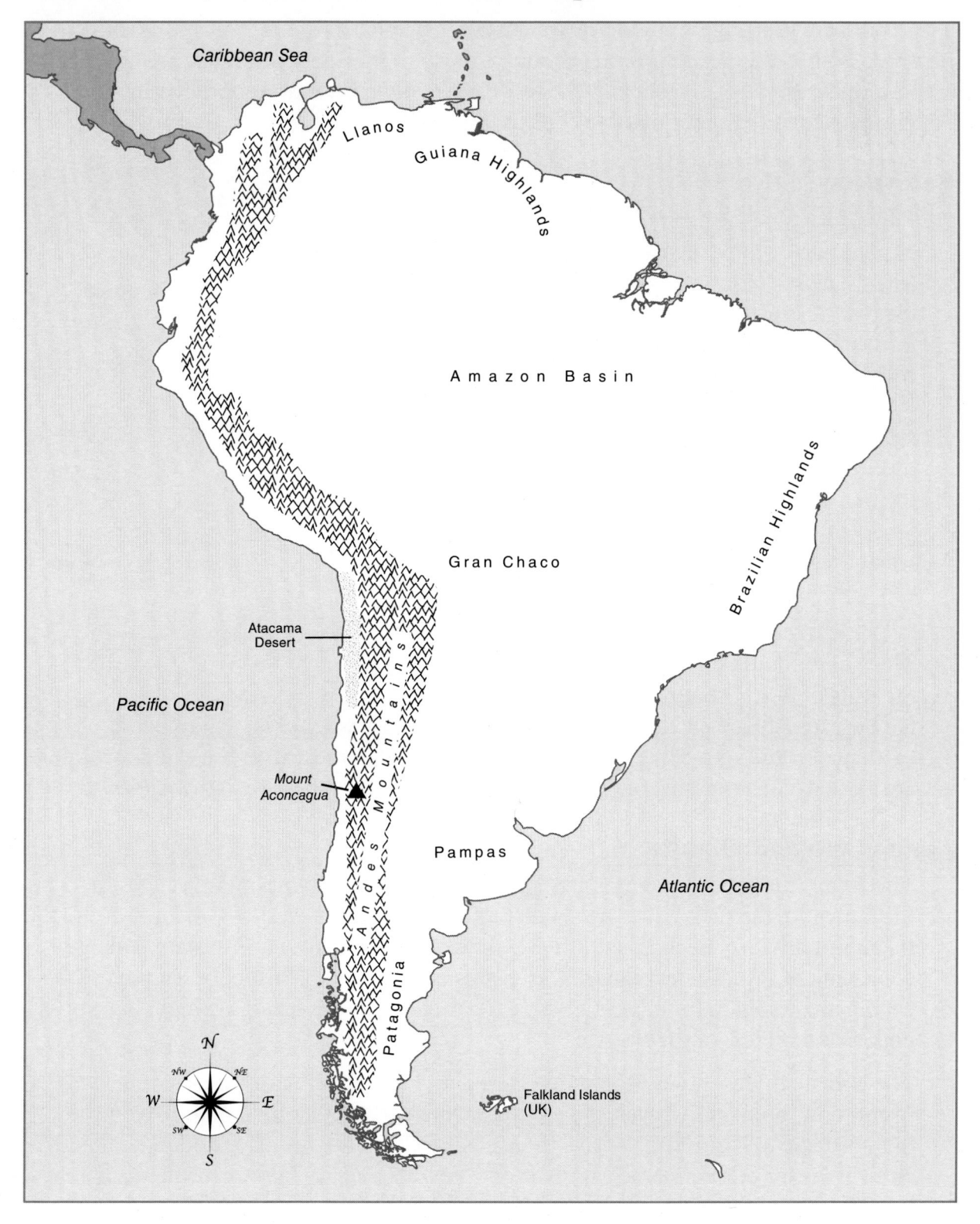

Name _____

Physical features

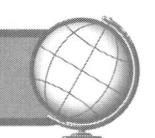

Andes Mountains

The Andes are the longest mountain system in the world, stretching 8851 km from northern South America almost to the southern tip of the continent. They are also the second-highest mountain system in the world. At 6960 m, Mount Aconcagua in Argentina is the tallest mountain in the Andes.

Formation

The Andes were formed millions of years ago by movements of *tectonic plates,* or large sections of the Earth's crust. The mountains formed when the Nazca Plate collided with the South American Plate. The Nazca Plate was *subducted,* meaning it sank below the South American Plate, and the Earth's surface was pushed up, forming the Andes. Today, when these plates move, they can cause violent earthquakes and volcanic eruptions.

The Andes Mountains are part of the Ring of Fire. The Ring of Fire is a huge area that encircles much of the Pacific Ocean, where a large number of earthquakes and volcanic eruptions take place. In fact, almost all of the world's volcanoes are located along the Ring of Fire. Over 200 of these volcanoes are in the Andes.

Landscape and Wildlife

The Andes mountain system is actually made up of several mountain ranges. In the far south, the mountains are smaller and do not rise above 3048 m. Further north, the mountains are much taller. In Peru and Bolivia, the mountain system widens, consisting of two different ranges with *plateaus* (high, flat plains) between them. The chain narrows again in the north where the mountains are still quite high, but not as high as the middle of the system.

The climate in the Andes Mountains is cold and harsh, yet many animals survive in this environment. Alpacas and vicuñas, which are related to llamas, live on the high plateaus. These animals have thick coats to keep them warm. Rodents called chinchillas make their homes in the rocky crevices and are known for their soft, thick fur. The Andean condor, a type of vulture, is the largest land bird in the Western Hemisphere. It feeds on *carrion* (dead animals) in the high mountain areas.

48 Exploring geography: South America   Prim-Ed Publishing   www.prim-ed.com

Andes Mountains

Tallest mountains in the Andes

	Mountain peak	Location	Height
1	Aconcagua	Argentina	6960 metres
2	Ojos del Salado	Argentina/Chile	6893 metres
3	Pissis	Argentina	6795 metres
4	Cerro Bonete	Argentina	6759 metres
5	Llullaillaco	Argentina/Chile	6739 metres
6	El Libertador	Argentina	6720 metres
6	Mercedario	Argentina/Chile	6720 metres
8	Huascarán	Peru	6713 metres
9	Tupungato	Argentina/Chile	6570 metres
10	Cachi	Argentina	6380 metres

Circle the correct answer for each clue. Use the information on page 48 and the chart above to help you.

1. the length of the Andes mountain system — **8851 km** / **9502 km**
2. the tallest mountain in the Andes — **Cerro Bonete** / **Aconcagua**
3. a mountain located in Peru — **Huascarán** / **Cachi**
4. a rodent that lives in the Andes — **chinchilla** / **vicuña**
5. the third-highest mountain in the Andes — **Mercedario** / **Pissis**
6. a type of vulture — **carrion** / **condor**
7. an animal related to llamas — **vicuña** / **chinchilla**
8. the second-tallest mountain in the Andes — **Aconcagua** / **Ojos del Salado**
9. a subducted tectonic plate — **South American** / **Nazca**
10. the area around the Pacific Ocean — **Ring of Volcanoes** / **Ring of Fire**

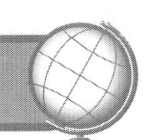

Highlands of South America

Guiana Highlands

The Guiana Highlands cover half of Venezuela, stretching from the southern part of the country across the northern edge of South America. The elevation of the Guiana Highlands ranges from less than 305 metres up to 2772 metres at its highest point, Mount Roraima. The most distinctive features of these highlands are sandstone plateaus with drop-offs that form steep cliffs. Because these formations look like tables, the land is often called *tablelands*. They are also called 'tepuis' by the local people. The word *tepui* means 'house of the gods'.

Tablelands of the Guiana Highlands

Brazilian Highlands

The Brazilian Highlands, also called the Brazilian Plateau, lie south-east of the Guiana Highlands. They are part of the same geological structure as the Guiana Highlands, but the two highlands have been separated from each other over time due to erosion by the Amazon River. The average elevation of the Brazilian Highlands is about 914 m. Rocky peaks occasionally dot the landscape, rising to 2743 m or more. Sugar Loaf peak, which rises steeply above Rio de Janeiro's harbour, is a famous feature of the Brazilian Highlands.

Patagonia

The Patagonian Plateau, often just called Patagonia, is located in Argentina and Chile and stretches south from the Pampas plains for 1609 km. Starting near the Atlantic Ocean, the land rises in step-like plateaus until it reaches the Andes Mountains in the west. These vast tablelands are desert or semidesert lands, meaning they receive very little rainfall. The ground in many places is covered with rounded pebbles, crumbling sandstone or lava.

Name _____

Physical features

Highlands of South America

A. Circle the correct answer for each question. Use the information on page 50 to help you.

1. Which highlands are located in the north? **Brazilian   Guiana**

2. Which highlands include Sugar Loaf peak? **Guiana   Brazilian**

3. Which highlands include desert land? **Patagonia   Guiana**

4. In which highlands is Rio de Janeiro located? **Brazilian   Patagonia**

5. Which highlands cover half of Venezuela? **Guiana   Brazilian**

6. Which highlands have a number of mountains that are over 2743 m high? **Patagonia   Brazilian**

7. In which highlands is the ground covered with rounded pebbles and lava? **Patagonia   Guiana**

B. Answer the questions. Use the information on page 50 to help you.

1. What is a tepui?

   _____

2. What does the word *tepui* mean in the local language?

   _____

3. What natural force separated the Guiana and Brazilian highlands?

   _____

4. In which countries is Patagonia located?

   _____

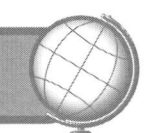

Plains of South America

Lowlands are level areas of land that are low in elevation. Plains are one type of South American lowlands. A plain is a large, mostly flat area that usually has few or no trees. There are three major plains regions in South America: the Llanos plains in the northern part of the continent, the Gran Chaco in the south-central part and the Pampas further south.

The chart below shows the three plains regions, their locations and facts about the lands.

KEY

▨ = Plains

Plains region	Approximate area	Location	Interesting facts
Llanos	570 000 sq. km	western Venezuela and north-eastern Colombia	• mostly rolling grassland with scattered trees • used for cattle grazing • warm temperatures year-round, at about 24 °C • one of the least-developed regions of South America
Gran Chaco	725 000 sq. km	parts of Argentina, Paraguay and Bolivia	• an arid grassland • rivers overrun banks and flood much of the area during rainy season • much of the land unused by people • name comes from the Quechua Indian word meaning 'hunting land'
The Pampas	764 000 sq. km	Central Argentina, most of Uruguay and southern Brazil	• fertile grasslands • heavily populated; used for farming and grazing • prone to frequent wildfires; keeps many trees from growing, even in fertile areas • home of the giant anteater, which grows to 2.1 m in length

Name _____

Physical features

Plains of South America

A. Write the name of the correct plains region to answer each question. Use the information on page 52 to help you.

1. Which plains region is the largest? _____

2. Which plains are located in Venezuela? _____

3. Which plains have frequent wildfires? _____

4. Which plains flood during the rainy season? _____

5. Which plains region has a temperature of about 24 °C all year long? _____

6. Which plains region is about 725 000 square kilometres? _____

7. Which region's name means 'hunting land' in the Quechua language? _____

8. In which plains do giant anteaters live? _____

9. Which plains are in one of the least developed regions of South America? _____

B. Answer the questions. Use the information on page 52 to help you.

1. What is a plain?

_____

_____

2. What is a lowland?

_____

_____

Name _____

Physical features

Amazon Rainforest

Much of South America is covered by tropical rainforests. Some of these forests are along the coast, but the largest rainforest area is located in the Amazon Basin. The Amazon Rainforest is the biggest tropical rainforest in the world.

The rainforest is divided into the following four layers:

1. The *emergent layer* includes the tallest trees that rise far above the rest of the vegetation. The treetops are exposed to rain and sunlight. Some animals spend their entire lives in these tall trees.

2. The next layer is the *canopy*. The trees in the canopy layer are so thick that they keep out about 80% of the sunlight from reaching the ground. Many other plants grow on the trees, and many animals live at this level.

3. The *understorey* gets very little sunlight. Most plants in the understory do not grow beyond 4 m tall.

4. The *forest floor* is littered with insects, small animals and decomposing plant matter. You would need a flashlight to explore this rainforest layer because it is so dark.

Amazon Rainforest facts

- The Amazon Rainforest covers about one-third of the continent.

- Scientists think the Amazon Rainforest is at least 55 million years old, making it one of the oldest tropical rainforests on the planet.

- The average temperature in the rainforest is 27 °C and it rains nearly every day.

- About 20% of the world's oxygen is produced in the Amazon Rainforest.

- There are more types of plants and animals in the Amazon Rainforest than anywhere else on Earth. There are over 40 000 different kinds of plants and more than 30 million species of insects. One-third of the world's birds can be found in the Amazon as well.

- Some of the more dangerous animals that live in the Amazon include the black caiman (an alligator-like reptile), the jaguar and the anaconda (a huge snake).

- Over 20% of the Amazon Rainforest has been destroyed. Many parts have been logged, while others have been cleared to create land for crops and for grazing livestock.

KEY
■ = Rainforests of South America

Name _____

Physical features

Amazon Rainforest

A. Complete each sentence by unscrambling the word under the line. Use the information on page 54 to help you.

1. The Amazon Rainforest covers about one-_____ of the continent.
   hidtr

2. The _____ layer is the highest part of the rainforest.
   gretenme

3. About 20% of the world's _____ comes from the Amazon Rainforest.
   yongex

4. There are over 30 million different species of _____ in the Amazon Rainforest.
   scinets

5. Many animals live in the _____ layer of the rainforest.
   pynoca

6. Black caimans, jaguars and _____ live in the Amazon.
   danascano

B. Label the four layers of the rainforest.

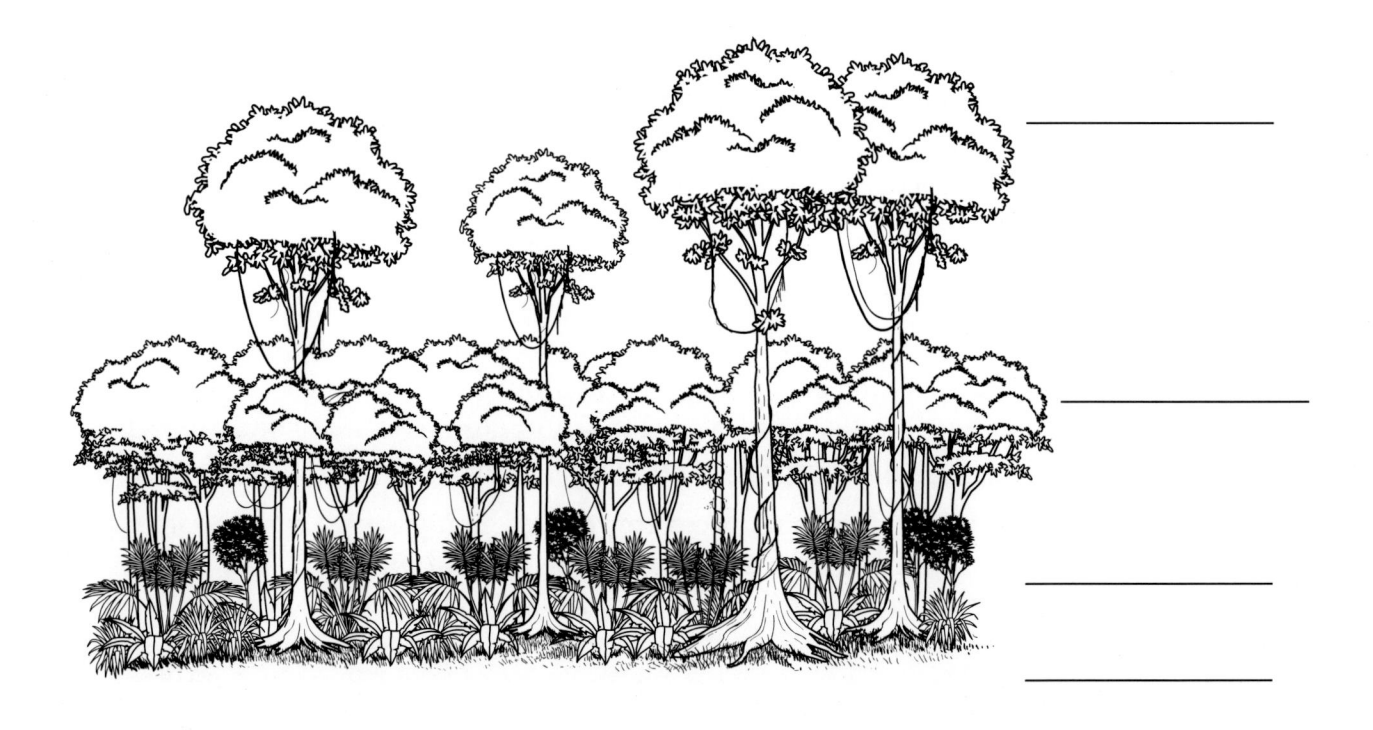

www.prim-ed.com   Prim-Ed Publishing   Exploring geography: South America   **55**

Name _____

Physical features

Atacama Desert

The Atacama Desert stretches 966 km through northern Chile. The desert is a high plateau that extends from the Pacific Ocean into the base of the Andes Mountains.

Driest place on Earth

Unlike most deserts, the Atacama is not hot. The average temperature is only about 19 °C. However, the region is considered a desert because it gets very little rain. In fact, the Atacama is thought to be the driest place on Earth. It gets less than 1.25 cm of rain a year. Many parts of the desert go for years without a single drop of rain. In fact, there are areas of the Atacama where rainfall has never been recorded!

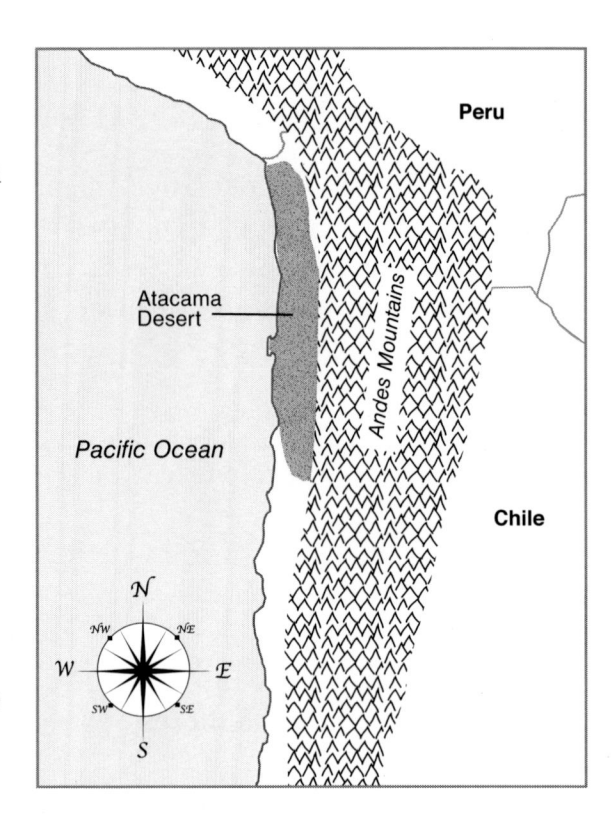

Why is the Atacama Desert so dry? The answer has to do with its location between the Andes Mountains and the Pacific Ocean.

The Atacama is located on the Pacific coast. Currents in the Pacific Ocean cause cold water from the depths of the ocean to move up to the surface. This cold water causes the air to be cold as well. The cold air creates fog and clouds, but no rain.

At the same time, moisture from warm, tropical air coming from the eastern part of the continent does not make it over the mountains to the Atacama. Instead, the air cools over the Andes. As it cools, moisture is released onto the eastern side of the mountains in the form of rain or snow. By the time the air reaches the desert on the other side of the mountains, it has lost most of its moisture. So the mountains that cause the Amazon Basin to collect so much rainfall are also responsible for keeping the Atacama so dry.

Desert terrain

Although it almost never rains, the fog in some parts of the Atacama provides enough moisture for algae, lichens and even some cacti to grow. There is some water stored underground, and there are also salty lakes. Flocks of flamingos live in and around the salt lakes. They feed on red algae that grow in the water.

Other than a few plants and animals, there are very few living things in the Atacama Desert. The terrain is mostly gravel, sand, salt basins and volcanic rock. The desert also contains rich deposits of copper and other metals.

Atacama Desert

A. Fill in the blanks to complete the paragraph about the Atacama Desert. Use the information on page 56 to help you.

The Atacama Desert is located in northern Chile between the Pacific Ocean and the _____ Mountains. The desert is the _____ place on Earth. Some places in the Atacama do not get any _____ for many years. Even though it rarely rains, the desert does get moisture from _____. Water can also be found stored _____ and in salt lakes. The terrain of the Atacama is mostly gravel, _____ rock, sand and salt basins. In addition, there are deposits of _____ as well as other metals in the desert.

B. Explain in your own words why the Atacama Desert is so dry.

_____
_____
_____
_____
_____

Name _____

Physical features

Tierra del Fuego

Tierra del Fuego is an *archipelago*, or a group of islands, located at the southern tip of South America. The name *Tierra del Fuego* means 'land of fire'. The islands were given that name in 1520 by Portuguese navigator Ferdinand Magellan when he saw from his ship the many fires that indigenous Indians had made to keep warm. Because the islands are so close to Antarctica, the climate of Tierra del Fuego is extremely cold.

The Tierra del Fuego archipelago is made up of one large island and many smaller ones. The main island, which is also called Tierra del Fuego, is divided between Argentina and Chile. The eastern side belongs to Argentina. The western side and all of the smaller islands belong to Chile. In the west, the Andes Mountains extend down to the small islands. The tallest mountain in Tierra del Fuego is Mount Darwin at 2438 m.

The route that Magellan sailed between Tierra del Fuego and the mainland of Chile is now called the Strait of Magellan. Although dangerous, it is much less treacherous than sailing around Cape Horn, the small island at the southernmost tip of Tierra del Fuego. The opening of the Panama Canal between North and South America in 1914 reduced the need for ships to use either of these routes.

A. Read each statement. Circle **yes** if it is true or **no** if it is false. Use the map on page 59 and the information above to help you.

1. An archipelago is a group of islands.   **Yes**   **No**

2. *Tierra del Fuego* means 'crown of fire'.   **Yes**   **No**

3. Tierra del Fuego is divided between Brazil and Chile.   **Yes**   **No**

4. All of the smaller islands belong to Chile.   **Yes**   **No**

5. Cape Horn is the southernmost part of the continent.   **Yes**   **No**

6. Tropical breezes keep the climate of the islands warm.   **Yes**   **No**

7. The Andes Mountains extend down to Tierra del Fuego.   **Yes**   **No**

8. Mount Darwin is the tallest mountain in Tierra del Fuego.   **Yes**   **No**

9. The Strait of Magellan connects the Pacific and Atlantic oceans.   **Yes**   **No**

Name _____

Physical features

Tierra del Fuego

B. Follow the directions for completing the map. Use the information on page 58 to help you.

1. Trace the dotted line that divides Argentina from Chile in red.
2. Label the island of Tierra del Fuego.
3. Label Cape Horn.
4. Label Mount Darwin.
5. Trace the route through the Strait of Magellan in blue.

C. How did Tierra del Fuego get its name?

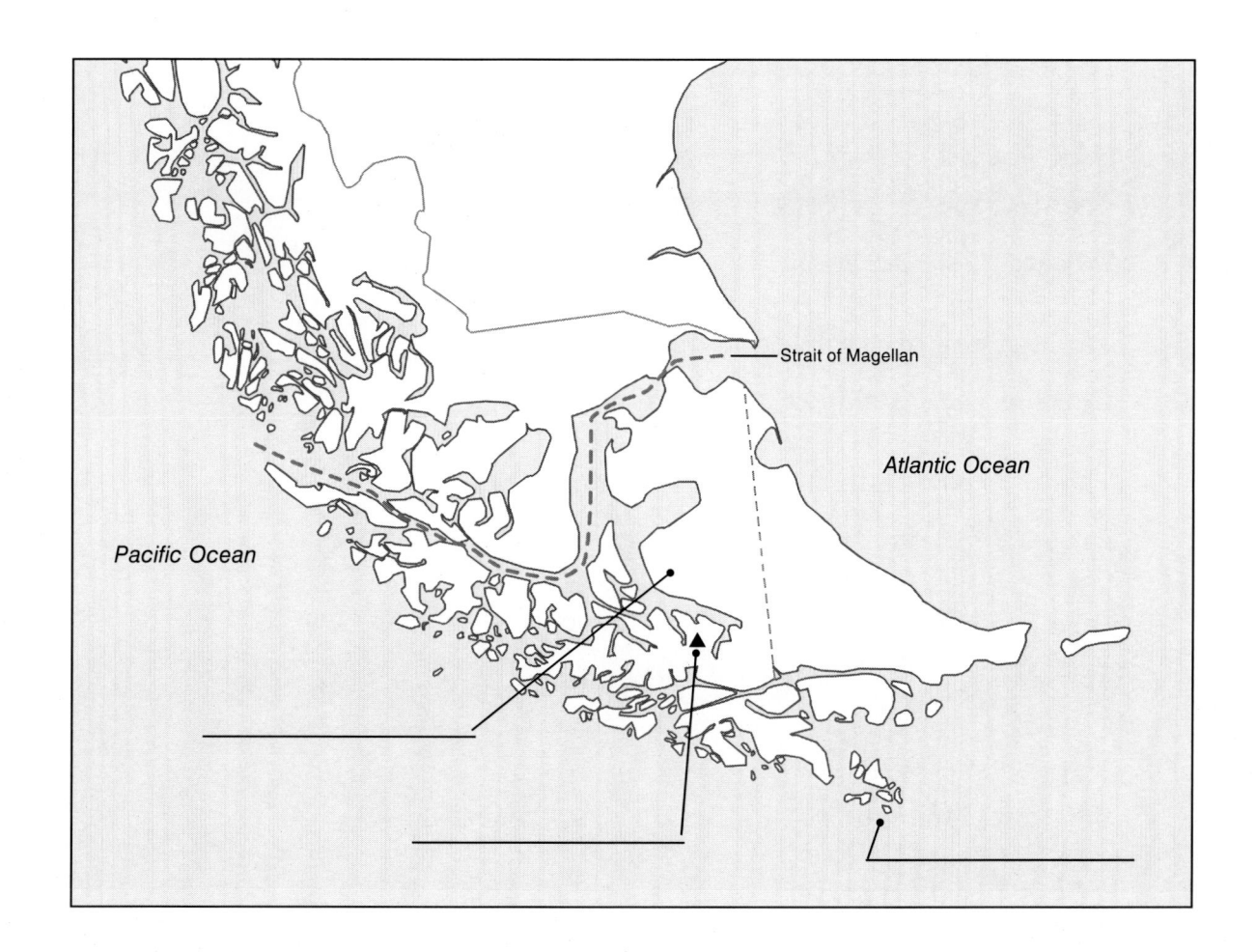

_____

_____

Name _____

Physical features

South America's bodies of water

The continent of South America is almost completely surrounded by water. The Pacific Ocean borders South America to the west and the Atlantic Ocean runs along the east. The Caribbean Sea is north of the continent. To the south, the Strait of Magellan separates Tierra del Fuego from the mainland. A *strait* is a narrow band of water that connects two larger bodies of water—in this case, the Pacific and Atlantic oceans.

Inland, several important river systems flow throughout South America. A river system is made up of all the rivers and *tributaries,* or streams that feed into larger rivers, that drain an area of land. The largest by far is the Amazon River system. The second-largest river system is made up of the Paraguay, Paraná and Uruguay rivers, all of which empty into the Atlantic Ocean at an area called Río de la Plata. The Orinoco River and its tributaries form the third-largest river system on the continent. Another important river is the São Francisco, which is located entirely within Brazil.

South America has very few lakes. The two largest lakes are Lake Titicaca in the west-central part of the continent, and Lake Maracaibo on the coast of Venezuela in the north.

A. Circle the correct word or words to complete each sentence. Use the information above and the map on page 61 to help you.

1. The Pacific Ocean is ___ of South America.

    east   **west**   **north**

2. The Strait of ___ connects the Pacific and Atlantic oceans.

    Titicaca   **del Fuego**   **Magellan**

3. The largest river system in South America is the ___.

    Amazon   **Orinoco**   **Paraguay**

4. The ___ River is located entirely within Brazil.

    Paraná   **São Francisco**   **Río de la Plata**

5. Lake ___ is located in the Andes Mountains.

    Maracaibo   **Titicaca**   **Orinoco**

6. Lake Maracaibo is located in ___.

    the Andes Mountains   **Brazil**   **Venezuela**

Name _____

Physical features

South America's bodies of water

B. Label the bodies of water on the map. Use the word box below and the information on page 60 to help you.

| Atlantic Ocean | Caribbean Sea | Lake Titicaca | Amazon River |
| Pacific Ocean | Strait of Magellan | Lake Maracaibo | |

Name _____

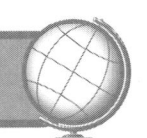

Physical features

Amazon River

The Amazon River is the longest river in South America and the second-longest river in the world. The Amazon begins high in the Andes Mountains in Peru, flows thousands of miles eastward and empties into the Atlantic Ocean.

Amazon River facts

- The Amazon River is over 6437 km. That is longer than the distance between London and Washington DC, in the USA!

- Even though the Amazon River is not quite the longest river in the world, it is by far the biggest in terms of volume of water. One-fifth of the water that flows into the oceans of the world comes from the Amazon.

- Most of the Amazon River flows through the tropical rainforests in Brazil.

- In some places, the Amazon River is so wide that a person standing on one bank cannot see the opposite shore. During the rainy season, the river can be up to 48 km across in some spots!

- The Amazon River floods every year, covering an area the size of Germany with water.

- Over 1000 tributaries flow into the Amazon River. Seven of these tributaries are over 1609 km long. The Madeira River is the longest tributary of the Amazon at 3351 km long.

- There are no bridges across the Amazon because there are few roads or cities in the Amazon Rainforest.

- Occasionally, an unusually high tide at the mouth of the river causes a large wave called a *tidal bore,* which travels rapidly upstream. A bore can reach heights of 4.6 m.

- A species of gigantic waterlily, called the *Victoria amazonica,* can be found in the shallow areas of the Amazon River. The round, floating leaves of this lily can reach nearly 3 m across and can support the weight of a small child.

- Over 2000 known kinds of fish live in the Amazon River system. Some scientists think there may be as many as 3500 species yet to be discovered.

Name _____

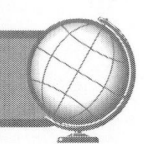

Physical features

Amazon River

Read each clue below. Write the correct word on the numbered lines. Then use the numbers to crack the code!

1. The Amazon River flows through the ____ rainforests in Brazil.

   $\overline{11}\ \overline{9}\ \overline{6}\ \overline{7}\ \overline{26}\ \overline{20}\ \overline{18}\ \overline{3}$

2. The Amazon River begins in the ____ Mountains.

   $\overline{18}\ \overline{5}\ \overline{21}\ \overline{22}\ \overline{10}$

3. The Madeira River is one of the seven longest ____ of the Amazon River.

   $\overline{11}\ \overline{9}\ \overline{26}\ \overline{19}\ \overline{12}\ \overline{11}\ \overline{18}\ \overline{9}\ \overline{26}\ \overline{22}\ \overline{10}$

4. Unusually high tides can cause a ____ to rush up the Amazon.

   $\overline{11}\ \overline{26}\ \overline{21}\ \overline{18}\ \overline{3}\ \ \overline{19}\ \overline{6}\ \overline{9}\ \overline{22}$

5. The *Victoria amazonica* is bigger than any other kind of ____ in the world.

   $\overline{1}\ \overline{18}\ \overline{11}\ \overline{22}\ \overline{9}\ \overline{3}\ \overline{26}\ \overline{3}\ \overline{8}$

6. The Amazon is the longest river in ____.

   $\overline{10}\ \overline{6}\ \overline{12}\ \overline{11}\ \overline{25}\ \ \overline{18}\ \overline{4}\ \overline{22}\ \overline{9}\ \overline{26}\ \overline{20}\ \overline{18}$

7. The Amazon River ends in the ____ Ocean.

   $\overline{18}\ \overline{11}\ \overline{3}\ \overline{18}\ \overline{5}\ \overline{11}\ \overline{26}\ \overline{20}$

Crack the code!

____, which are native to the Amazon River, are known for their ferocious appetites.

$\overline{7}\ \overline{26}\ \overline{9}\ \overline{18}\ \overline{5}\ \overline{25}\ \overline{18}\ \overline{10}$

Name _____

Physical features

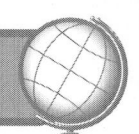

Lake Titicaca

Lake Titicaca is the largest lake in South America. At 3810 m above sea level, it is also one of the highest lakes in the world. The lake is located high in the Andes Mountains and straddles the border between Peru and Bolivia. It is 193 km long and 81 km wide. Lake Titicaca has an average depth of about 183 m. Its deepest part is 280 m in the north-east corner.

More than 25 rivers drain into Lake Titicaca. Only one small river, the Desaguadero, drains out of the lake.

Lake Titicaca is split into two bodies of water, one much larger than the other. They are joined by a strait. The lake is dotted with 41 islands, some of them heavily populated. The largest is Titicaca Island (also called Isla del Sol). It is part of the country of Bolivia.

Two native species of fish live in Lake Titicaca. One is the small, black-striped killifish, and the other is a type of catfish. There are also trout that were brought to the lake in the late 1930s for fishing. A large species of frog that can reach up to 50 cm in length also lives in Lake Titicaca.

A. Write the letter of the clue that describes each term. Use the information above and the map on page 65 to help you.

_____ 1. Bolivia

_____ 2. Desaguadero

_____ 3. Isla del Sol

_____ 4. killifish

_____ 5. trout

_____ 6. 193 km

_____ 7. 183 m

_____ 8. Peru

a. the only river that drains out of Lake Titicaca

b. a fish native to Lake Titicaca

c. the country on the western side of Lake Titicaca

d. the average depth of Lake Titicaca

e. a fish that was brought to Lake Titicaca in the 1930s

f. the country on the eastern side of Lake Titicaca

g. the length of Lake Titicaca

h. the largest island in Lake Titicaca

Name _____

Physical features

Lake Titicaca

B. Write a caption for the map. Use the information on page 64 to help you.

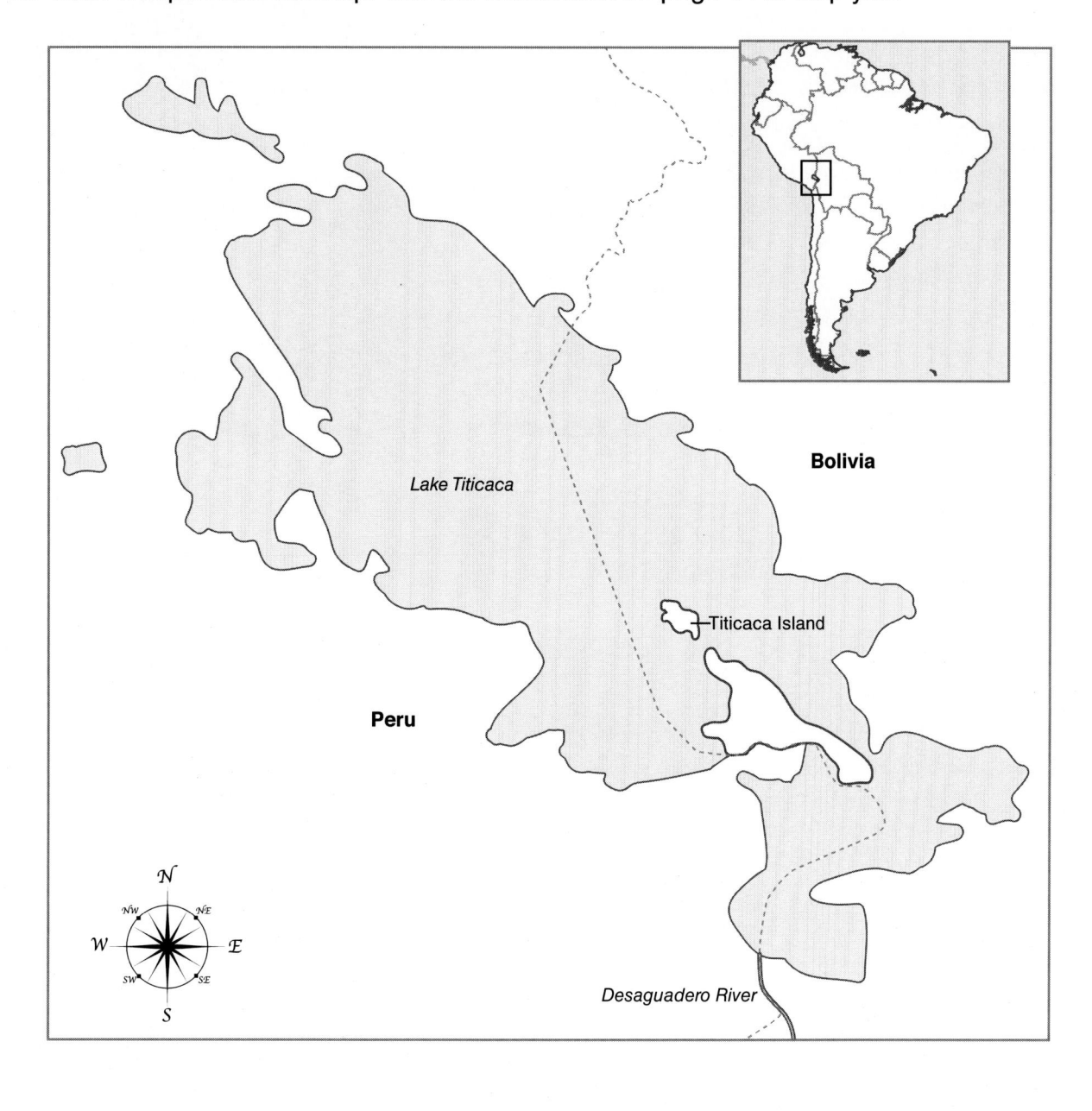

_____

_____

_____

Name _____

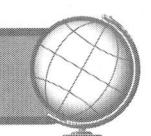

Physical features

Angel Falls

Angel Falls is the highest waterfall in the world. It is located on the Churun River in the Guiana Highlands of Venezuela. The river flows over a flat-topped mountain called Auyantepui and plunges 979 m to the bottom.

Angel Falls was named for Jimmie Angel, an American pilot who was the first person to fly over the falls in an airplane. Another name for the falls is *Kerepakupai merú*. This name, given by natives, means 'waterfall of the deepest place'.

Angel Falls is surrounded by dense rainforest, making it difficult for tourists to visit. In order to see the falls, most visitors travel by plane to a camp. There, they can take a boat up the river to the bottom of the falls. Other people fly by the falls in an airplane. However, if the day is cloudy, they may not get to see the falls at all.

A. Answer each question. Use the information above to help you.

1. Where is Angel Falls located? Be specific.

   _____

2. How did Angel Falls get its name?

   _____

3. What does *Kerepakupai merú* mean?

   _____

B. Would you want to visit Angel Falls? Why or why not?

_____

_____

Name _____

Review

Use words from the box to complete the crossword puzzle.

Word box:
Amazon
Andes
Atacama
Guiana
Patagonia
plateau
Rainforest
strait

Across

3. The _____ River runs from the Andes Mountains into the Atlantic Ocean.

5. The _____ Highlands are located in northern South America.

7. the longest mountain system in the world

8. a narrow band of water that connects two larger bodies of water

Down

1. a vast area of dry tablelands in southern Argentina

2. Over 40 million plants can be found in the Amazon _____.

4. a mostly flat highland

6. The _____ Desert is the driest place on Earth.

SECTION 4

Valuable resources of South America

In this section, pupils learn about the various natural resources of South America. They discover that hydropower, oil and mining are all important industries in South America. They also learn about regional crops and cattle production. In addition, pupils learn about resources of the rainforest and some of the interesting animals of South America.

CONTENTS

Overview 70–71	Llamas and alpacas 82–83
Oil in Venezuela 72–73	Rainforest resources 84–85
Itaipú Dam 74–75	Amazon Rainforest wildlife 86–87
Mining metals 76–77	Galápagos Islands wildlife 88–89
Agriculture 78–79	Review 90
Cattle 80–81	

Name _____

Valuable resources

Overview

Natural resources are the minerals, plants, animals and other elements that humans use from their environment. South America is rich in many kinds of natural resources. There are large deposits of oil, as well as many types of minerals. Thousands of different plants and animals are found in South America's rainforests, and many crops are planted and livestock raised in various regions of the continent.

Energy

South America relies on both oil and hydropower (the force of moving water) for its energy needs. There are large deposits of oil in Venezuela, much of which is exported to other countries. The rivers of South America produce hydropower at large plants, such as the one located at the Itaipú Dam on the Paraná River.

Mining

South America's land is rich in many kinds of minerals. Valuable metals such as copper, iron, lead, tin and mercury are mined in South America. In fact, the largest copper mine in the world is the Escondida mine in Chile.

Farming

South America grows large crops of wheat, soybeans and corn. There are also many smaller 'specialty' crops grown. These include bananas, coffee beans, kiwis, mangos, pineapples, quinoa and peppers.

Much of South America's land is used for livestock. Both Brazil and Argentina produce large numbers of cattle. In the Andes Mountains, llamas are raised for use as pack animals, and alpacas are raised for their wool, which is made into warm clothing.

Forests

More than 40% of South America is covered by rainforest. The rainforest is home to thousands of different kinds of plants and animals. People use a variety of rainforest resources for food, medicines and wood. Unfortunately, each year more rainforest is cut down to make room for grazing livestock.

Animals

South America is home to many interesting types of wildlife. The rainforest is full of reptiles such as the green anaconda, mammals such as the capybara and sloth, and fish such as the piranha. The Galápagos Islands are home to many animals that cannot be found anywhere else in the world. These include the Galápagos tortoise, the Galápagos penguin and the marine iguana.

Name _____

Valuable resources

Overview

Tick the correct box to answer each question.

1. The large hydropower plant located on the Paraná River is part of which South American dam?
   - ☐ Atacama
   - ☐ Itaipú
   - ☐ Galápagos
   - ☐ Escondida

2. Which country produces the most copper?
   - ☐ Venezuela
   - ☐ Brazil
   - ☐ Peru
   - ☐ Chile

3. Which of these is a specialty crop of South America?
   - ☐ peppers
   - ☐ wheat
   - ☐ soybeans
   - ☐ corn

4. About how much of South America is covered by rainforest?
   - ☐ 50%
   - ☐ 40%
   - ☐ 30%
   - ☐ 20%

5. Which of these animals lives in the Galápagos Islands?
   - ☐ sloth
   - ☐ capybara
   - ☐ marine iguana
   - ☐ anaconda

Name _____

Valuable resources

Oil in Venezuela

Oil is a *fossil fuel*. This means that it was formed from the remains of animals and plants that lived millions of years ago. These remains were covered by layers of soil. Over time, heat and pressure turned the remains into what is called *crude oil*.

Crude oil is a yellowish black liquid that is usually found in underground reservoirs. A well is drilled into the reservoir to bring the crude oil to the surface. The oil is then sent to a refinery, or factory, where it is separated into usable products such as gasoline, diesel fuel and heating oil.

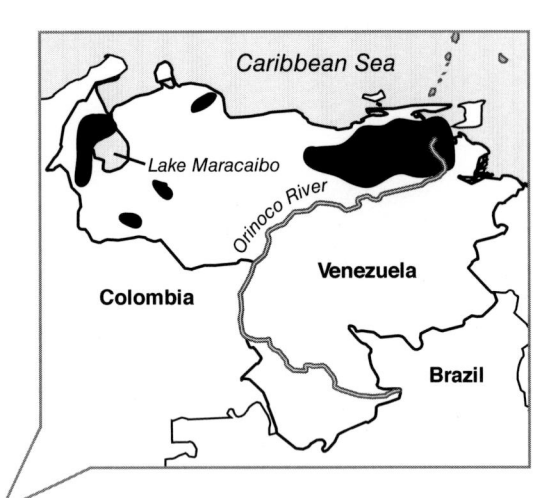

Several countries in South America have large crude oil deposits, including Colombia, Ecuador, Peru and Brazil. But the largest deposits are located in Venezuela. Venezuela is one of the top 10 oil-producing countries in the world, with oil fields near Lake Maracaibo and along the Orinoco River. Venezuela exports about three-quarters of its oil to other countries.

Venezuela's oil production
1980–2008

Year	Barrels per day
1980	2 246 000
1984	1 872 000
1988	2 008 000
1992	2 520 000
1996	3 175 000
2000	3 460 000
2004	2 855 000
2008	2 643 000

KEY
■ = oil deposits

Name _____

Valuable resources

Oil in Venezuela

A. Use the information and the map on page 72 to answer the questions.

1. What four countries in South America, besides Venezuela, have large deposits of oil?

   _____

2. In which two areas is most of the oil in Venezuela located?

   _____

3. About how much of Venezuela's oil is exported? _____

4. In what year did Venezuela produce the most oil? _____

B. Use the information in the chart on page 72 to create a line graph showing Venezuela's oil production from 1980 to 2008. First, make a dot for each year to show the number of barrels per day. (You will need to estimate where the dot goes between the numbers along the line.) Then use a ruler to connect the dots.

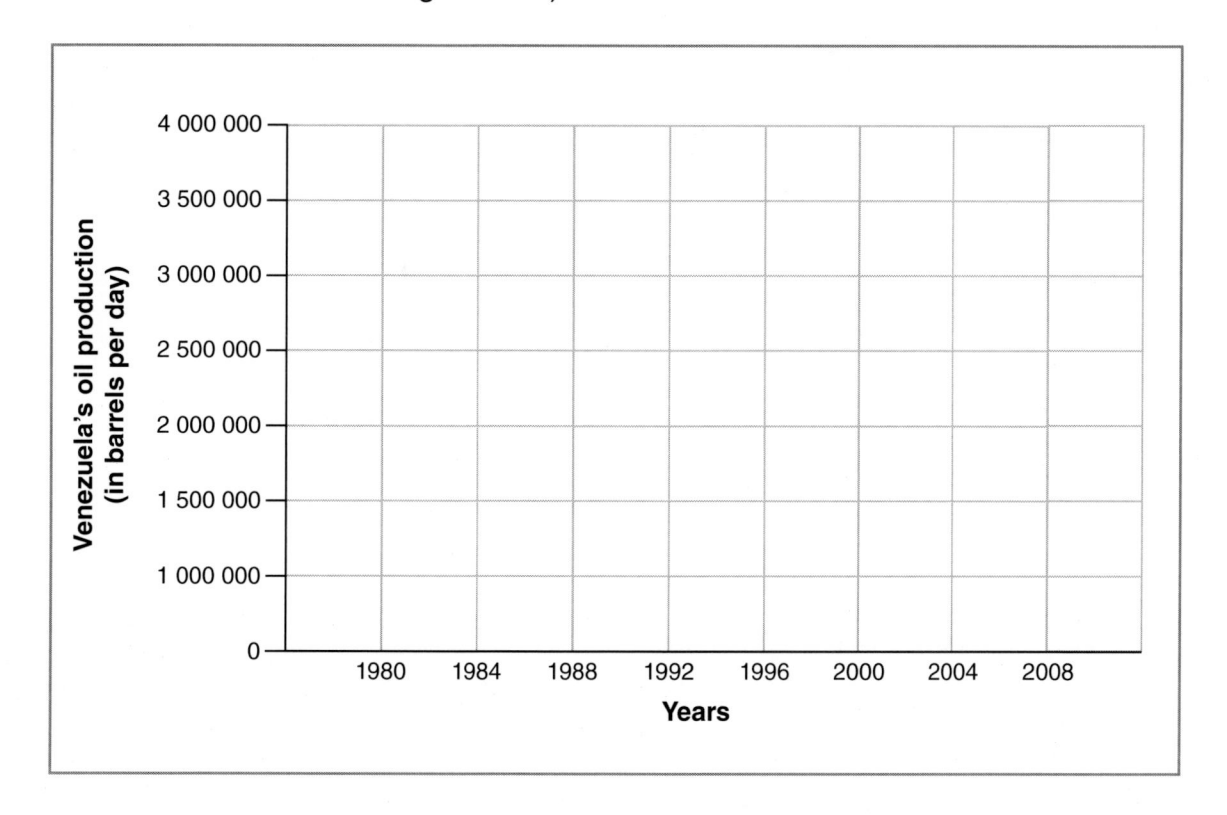

[Line graph with y-axis labeled "Venezuela's oil production (in barrels per day)" ranging from 0 to 4 000 000 in increments of 500 000, and x-axis labeled "Years" with values 1980, 1984, 1988, 1992, 1996, 2000, 2004, 2008]

www.prim-ed.com   Prim-Ed Publishing   Exploring geography: South America   73

Itaipú Dam

The Itaipú Dam is one of the largest dams in the world. It is also the largest producer of *hydroelectricity* on the planet. Hydroelectricity is generated by the force of moving water. The dam is located on the Paraná River on the border between Paraguay and Brazil. It supplies about 94% of Paraguay's electricity and about 20% of Brazil's.

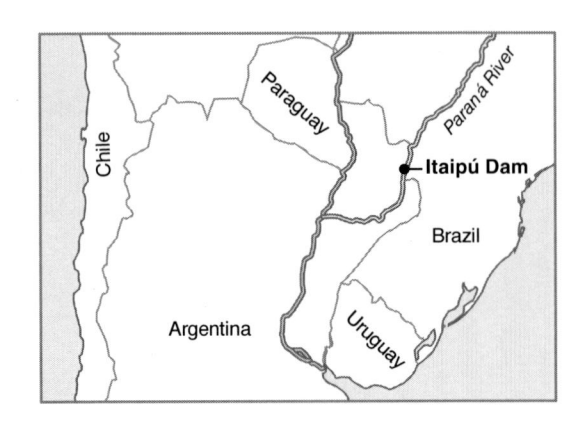

Rerouting the Paraná River

In order to build the Itaipú Dam, the Paraná River had to be temporarily rerouted around the construction site. Rerouting the seventh-largest river in the world was not an easy task. Workers started digging a 2.1 kilometre-long canal for the river's new route in 1975 and did not finish until 1978. They removed around 45 million tonnes of earth to create the canal, which was 91 m deep and nearly 152 m wide.

The Itaipú Dam stretches nearly 8 km across the Paraná River and is 196 m tall—about the height of a 65-story building.

Construction

About 40 000 workers were needed to construct the dam. The main part of the dam was built with large concrete blocks. The blocks were put together to form a hollow chamber inside. Enough iron and steel was used to build 380 Eiffel Towers!

Before the dam could be used, thousands of people who lived near the river had to be relocated. The dam caused the river to spread out into a large *reservoir,* or lake of stored water, that is over 161 km long.

Once the dam was completed, work on the powerhouse could begin. The powerhouse contains 20 giant hydroelectric generators. These generators use the force of the water coming through the dam to make electricity.

Name _____

Valuable resources

Itaipú Dam

A. Complete each sentence by unscrambling the word below each line. Use the information on page 74 to help you.

Some of the answers will need to start with capital letters.

1. The Itaipú Dam is located on the _____ River.
   anarpa

2. The dam supplies about 94% of _____'s electricity.
   grapayau

3. The Paraná River is the _____-largest river in the world.
   vestehn

4. Most of the dam is made from huge _____ blocks.
   trenecoc

5. The dam caused the river to spread into a giant _____.
   veesirror

6. There are 20 hydroelectric _____ in the powerhouse.
   stranegreo

7. The generators use the force of the _____ to make electricity.
   wreat

B. Write the letter of the clue that describes each number. Use the information on page 74 to help you.

____ 1. 40 000   a. the width of the Paraná River bypass

____ 2. 152 km   b. the number of workers who constructed the dam

____ 3. 161 km   c. the approximate amount of earth removed to create the bypass

____ 4. 2.1 km   d. the length of the Paraná River bypass

____ 5. 8 km   e. the height of the Itaipú Dam

____ 6. 45 million tonnes f. the length of the reservoir created by the Itaipú Dam

____ 7. 196 m   g. the length of the Itaipú Dam

Name _____

Valuable resources

Mining metals

Copper

South America is one of the leading producers of copper. A good portion of that copper comes from Chile, which exports more copper than any other country in the world. In fact, about 30% of the world's copper comes from Chile.

Most of the rich deposits of copper in Chile are found in the northern part of the country in the Atacama Desert. The largest copper mine in the world, Escondida, is located there. Over 900 000 tonnes of copper are mined each year from two giant pits in Escondida. About 4000 people work at the mine.

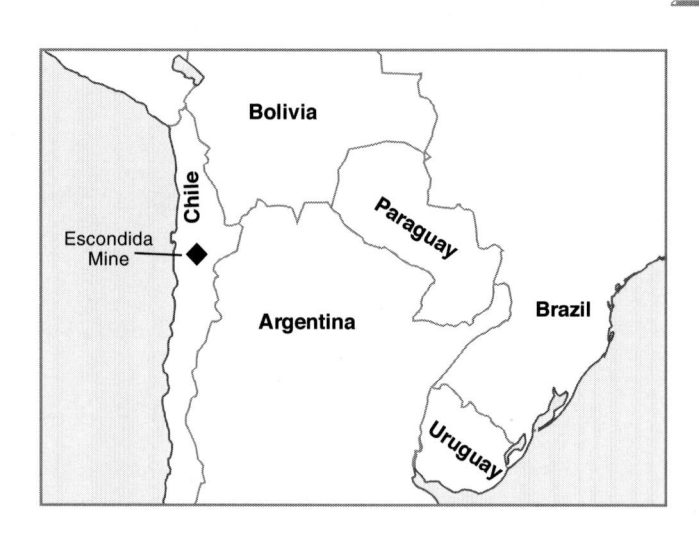

Copper is in high demand because it is easy to shape and it conducts, or carries, heat and electricity very well. Copper is used to make electrical wire and is found in motors, generators, computer circuit boards and pipes, as well as in pots and pans. Copper can also be combined with other metals to make *alloys,* or mixtures of two or more metals, such as bronze and brass.

Fill in the blanks to complete the paragraphs on copper. Use the information above to help you.

_____ supplies about 30% of the world's copper.

The largest copper mine in the world, _____,

is located in the _____ Desert. About 4000 workers

mine the copper from two large _____.

Copper is used to make wire because it is a good conductor of heat and

_____. Copper can also be combined with other metals

to make _____ such as bronze and brass.

76 Exploring geography: South America — Prim-Ed Publishing www.prim-ed.com

Name _____

Valuable resources

Mining metals

Other metals

Many other metals besides copper are mined in South America. The chart below lists the other metals mined in South America and describes their uses.

Metal	Countries	Uses
Bauxite (Aluminum)	Brazil, Guyana and Suriname	used to make aircraft, rocket and automobile parts, as well as aluminum foil and cans
Iron	Argentina, Brazil, Chile, Colombia, Peru and Venezuela	used to make machinery, tools, automobiles, ships and building materials
Lead	Argentina, Bolivia and Peru	used in pipes, roofing materials, batteries and bullets; used as a shield from radiation, such as from X-ray machines
Manganese	Argentina, Bolivia, Brazil, Chile, Ecuador and Uruguay	used to make the alloy steel
Mercury	Chile and Peru	used in barometers, fluorescent lights and batteries
Molybdenum	Chile and Peru	used to make aircraft and missile parts, filaments in light bulbs, and in nuclear power production
Tin	Bolivia and Brazil	used to make cans for storing food; combined with copper to make the alloy bronze
Zinc	Argentina, Bolivia and Peru	used to protect iron and steel from rusting

Circle the correct metal for each clue. Use the chart above to help you.

1. This metal is mined in Venezuela.   **iron**   **manganese**

2. This metal is used to make fluorescent lights.   **bauxite**   **mercury**

3. This metal can protect you from radiation.   **lead**   **zinc**

4. This metal is mined in Chile.   **molybdenum**   **bauxite**

5. This metal is used to make food containers.   **mercury**   **tin**

6. This metal protects iron from rusting.   **bauxite**   **zinc**

7. This metal is used to make the alloy steel.   **manganese**   **tin**

Name _____

Valuable resources

Agriculture

Although there are large farms in South America, most of the farms are on small plots of land called *minifundios*. These small farms are usually run by a single family. They rely on traditional farming methods—humans and animals do the work, not machines.

Many different kinds of crops are grown in South America. The continent is a leading producer of corn, soybeans and wheat. Other popular crops include beans, rice and potatoes. Ecuador is the world's top banana producer and Colombia and Brazil produce a lot of coffee beans. In addition to these crops, many smaller specialty crops are grown in South America, including brazil nuts, quinoa (KEEN-wah) and peppers.

Brazil nuts

Brazil nuts come from one of the largest trees in the Amazon Rainforest. They cannot be grown in orchards because they depend on certain species of rainforest bees for pollination. Brazil nuts are actually the tree's seeds. They grow in hard shells inside a large pod that looks like a coconut.

Brazil nuts

South America produces about 18 000 tonnes of Brazil nuts a year. Most of these nuts come from Bolivia, but they are also harvested in Brazil and Peru.

Quinoa

Although it looks like a grain, quinoa is the seed of the goosefoot plant. It grows at high altitudes in the Andes Mountains. Quinoa has been grown by native peoples for over 5000 years. The Incas called it the 'mother grain'.

Quinoa is high in protein and minerals and is easy to digest. It is commonly boiled and used as an alternative to rice. South America produces about 54 tonnes of quinoa each year. Peru is the highest producer of quinoa, followed by Bolivia and Ecuador.

goosefoot plant

Peppers

Many varieties of peppers are grown in South America. Some peppers, such as green, red and yellow peppers, are mild. Others, such as jalapeño and cayenne peppers are spicy. These hot peppers are often called chilli peppers. Peppers have been used in South American cuisine for thousands of years.

peppers

Brazil is the biggest producer of peppers, harvesting nearly 65 000 tonnes of peppers each year. Other pepper-producing countries include Ecuador, Bolivia and Peru.

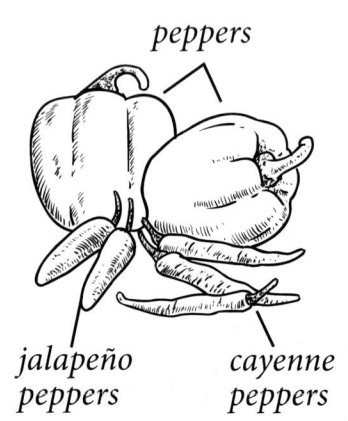

jalapeño peppers   *cayenne peppers*

Name _____

Valuable resources

Agriculture

A. Read each statement. Circle **yes** if it is true or **no** if it is false. Use the information on page 78 to help you.

1. Large farms in South America are called minifundios.   Yes   No

2. Small family farms rely on human and animal labour.   Yes   No

3. Soybeans are an important crop in South America.   Yes   No

4. Brazil produces more bananas than any other country.   Yes   No

5. Coffee beans are grown in Colombia.   Yes   No

6. More Brazil nuts come from Brazil than any other country.   Yes   No

7. Brazil produces almost 65 000 tonnes of quinoa each year.   Yes   No

8. Quinoa grows in Peru.   Yes   No

B. Write the correct crop—*Brazil nuts, quinoa* or *peppers*—for each clue.

1. This crop grows at high altitudes.   _____

2. This crop has hot and mild varieties.   _____

3. This crop has yellow, green and red varieties.   _____

4. This crop grows on trees in the rainforest.   _____

5. This crop looks like a grain, but it is not one.   _____

6. This crop grows in hard pods.   _____

C. Circle the foods from South America that you have tried. Make a star by the ones that you liked.

| bananas | Brazil nuts | jalapeño peppers | beans |
| quinoa | potatoes | peppers | rice |

www.prim-ed.com   Prim-Ed Publishing   Exploring geography: South America   79

Name _____

Valuable resources

Cattle

Much of South America's climate and terrain is ideal for raising cattle. Cattle are raised both for dairy or milk products, and for beef production. By far the greatest numbers of cattle in South America are beef cattle. Brazil and Argentina are world leaders in the cattle industry.

Argentina has a long history of cattle raising. About 75% of Argentina's cattle are raised on the grassy Pampas lowlands, which are perfect for grazing. The cattle industry in Argentina produces about 55 million cattle each year. Argentina has the world's highest rate of beef consumption. The average amount eaten per person each year is 70 kg.

In contrast, Brazil's cattle industry has been growing rapidly since the early 1970s. Today, there are about 190 million cattle in Brazil. The increase in cattle has depended on continually finding new land for grazing. This has resulted in large areas of rainforest being destroyed to make room for the cattle.

Cattle production in Argentina and Brazil

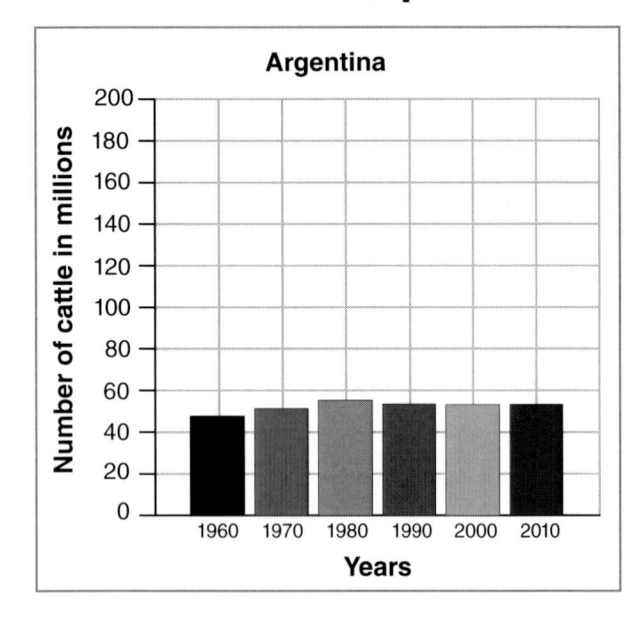

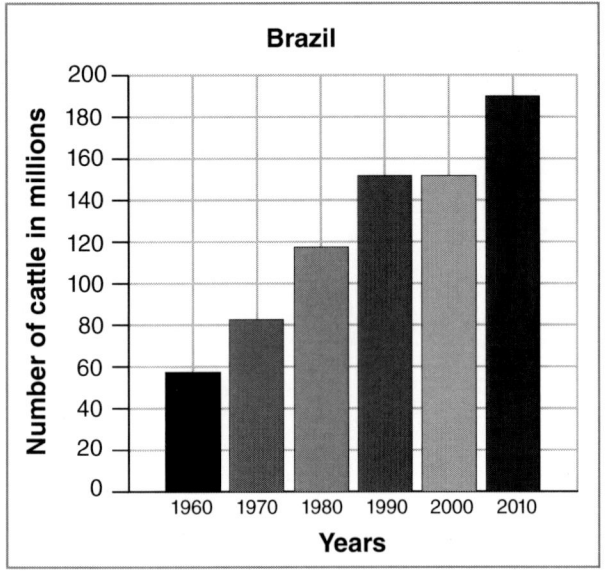

80   Exploring geography: South America   Prim-Ed Publishing   www.prim-ed.com

Name _____

Valuable resources

Cattle

A. Read each statement. Circle **yes** if it is true or **no** if it is false. Use the information and graphs on page 80 to help you.

1. Brazil and Peru are world leaders in the cattle industry. Yes No

2. The Pampas is home to about 75% of the cattle in Argentina. Yes No

3. More cattle are raised in Brazil than in Argentina. Yes No

4. Argentina's cattle industry is not growing or declining. Yes No

5. Argentina had more cattle than Brazil in 1960. Yes No

6. Argentina had fewer cattle in 1980 than in 2000. Yes No

7. Brazil's cattle population grew by about 40 million between 2000 and 2010. Yes No

8. Today, Brazil has more than three times as many cattle as Argentina. Yes No

B. Write three sentences about cattle production in Argentina and Brazil, using the information in the graph on page 80.

1. _____

2. _____

3. _____

Name _____

Valuable resources

Llamas and alpacas

Llamas and alpacas are important herd animals in South America. They are members of the camel family and were domesticated (tamed) by the Incas thousands of years ago. These animals can no longer be found in the wild, but their relatives, the guanaco and vicuña, can be.

Llama

Alpaca

Location
- raised primarily in Bolivia, Peru, Ecuador, Chile and Argentina

Characteristics
- can reach 113 kg
- usually white, but can also be black or brown
- long neck and legs, short tail, small head and coarse hair

Diet
- grazes on grasses and other plants
- can go long periods without water

Behaviour
- usually gentle and curious
- will sometimes spit, kick or refuse to move when mistreated

Use by people
- primarily used as a pack animal in the rugged Andes
- can be sheared; wool used to make rugs, rope and fabric

Location
- raised in central and southern Peru and western Bolivia

Characteristics
- can reach 64 kg
- usually black or brown, but can also be light grey, tan or occasionally white
- long neck and legs, short tail and small head
- soft, warm coat, which grows to touch the ground if it is not sheared

Diet
- grazes on grasses and other plants

Behaviour
- usually gentle and curious
- gets upset when separated from herd

Use by people
- valued for its remarkably soft and warm wool, which is made into jackets, jumpers and other cold-weather clothing

Name _____

Valuable resources

Llamas and alpacas

A. Read each statement below. Write the letter of each statement in the correct space on the Venn diagram. Use the information on page 82 to help you.

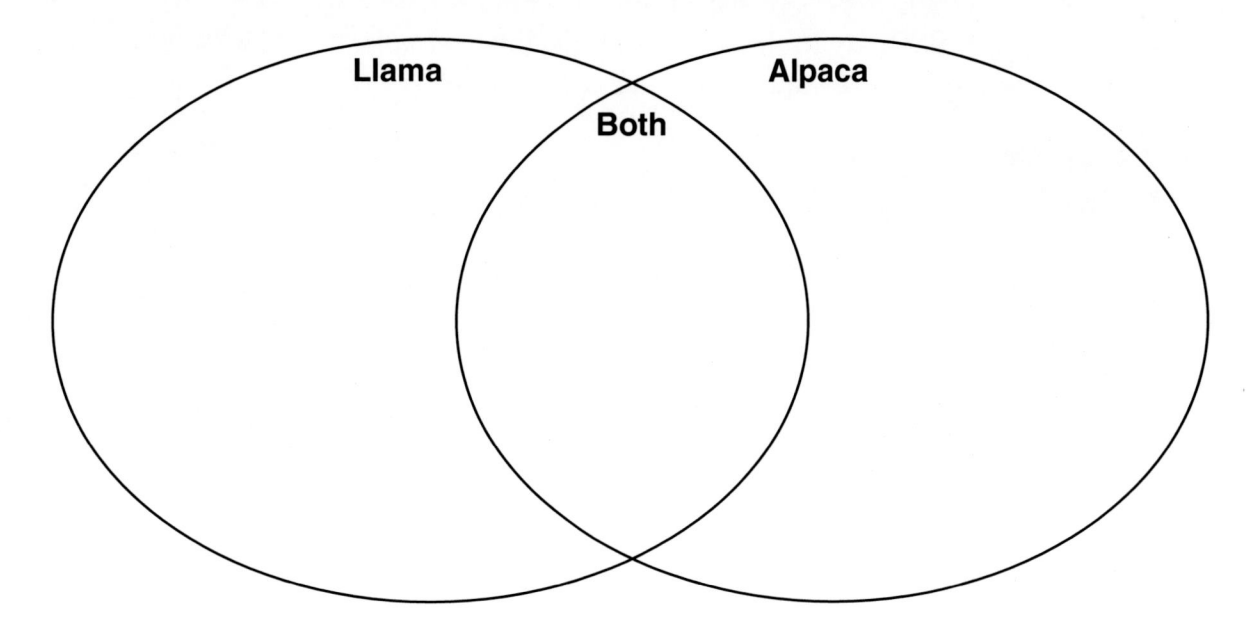

Llama | Both | Alpaca

A. used mostly as a pack animal

B. can weigh up to 64 kg

C. has a soft, warm coat

D. is a domesticated herd animal

E. cannot be found in the wild

F. has a coarse coat

G. is usually white

H. can be found in Chile

I. is gentle and curious

J. is usually black or brown

B. If you lived in the Andes Mountains and your family kept a herd of animals, would you rather have alpacas or llamas? Explain your answer.

_____
_____
_____

Rainforest resources

More than 40% of the land in South America is covered by rainforest. There are more living things in the rainforests of South America than anywhere else on Earth. Thousands of plants and animals thrive in the warm, humid climate. Many of these plants and animals are important resources for people.

KEY
■ = Rainforests

Herbs and medicines

Native South Americans have been using plants from the rainforest to cure illnesses for thousands of years. Only recently have scientists in the rest of the world come to understand the value and importance of rainforest plants.

One of the first discoveries was that a medicine called *quinine* could be made from the bark of a certain rainforest tree. Quinine is used to treat malaria, a sometimes deadly disease that is spread by mosquitoes in tropical countries. Today, many scientists believe that rainforest plants could hold the cures for flus, viruses, cancer and AIDs. However, there is a great deal of work to be done. Scientists have examined only about 1% of rainforest plants for use in treating illnesses.

Air, water and food

The Amazon Rainforest has been called the 'lungs of the world' because the trees and other plants there produce about 20% of the world's oxygen. In addition, the Amazon Basin holds about one-fifth of the world's supply of fresh water. The rainforest is also rich in edible vegetation. Many foods that we eat every day were first found in the Amazon Rainforest. These include avocados, coconuts, figs, oranges, lemons, mangos, grapefruit, bananas, pineapples, chocolate, ginger, coffee and several kinds of nuts.

Wood

Many kinds of *hardwoods* are found in the Amazon Rainforest. Hardwoods are used to make furniture, musical instruments, boats and even coffins. Some of these hardwoods include teak, rosewood and mahogany. Rainforest trees are also cut to make lumber for construction and charcoal. Unfortunately, both legal and illegal logging is destroying many of South America's rainforests.

Grazing land

Rainforest land itself is also valuable. It is often wanted to make more room for grazing animals. This demand for farm land has resulted in many rainforests being cleared using the 'slash and burn' method. This method involves using fire to destroy all of the trees and other plants on the land. None of the valuable wood and resources are saved. Over 29 785 square km of South American rainforests are cleared in this way every year.

Name _____

Valuable resources

Rainforest resources

A. Find and circle the rainforest resources in the word puzzle. Words may appear across, down or diagonally.

```
A B I W A T T B A N A N A S D
M Y B Y F I N D B C F B T H E
R N Q M T S L O W V M I E A M
A N U M O R T W H A R E G L A
Y L I G C U K S N F T M W S H
B R N T H E O R E I S E N T O
H A I I N G A G I C A N R X G
M D N P A B V O U T K P A D A
D E E W H Q O X Y G E N C A N
T A Y U N E C I S A P I H V Y
R E I T C K A D A M M U E I B
W L A N E Y D V E R S Q L D I
L A G K I W O L H A V E G O S
E A X D R O S E W O O D S M G
```

| avocados |
| bananas |
| figs |
| mahogany |
| mangos |
| oxygen |
| quinine |
| rosewood |
| teak |
| water |

B. Choose three of the resources listed in the word box above. Use each one in a sentence explaining how you have used that resource in your life.

1. _____

2. _____

3. _____

Name _____

Valuable resources

Amazon Rainforest wildlife

Every part of the Amazon Rainforest, from the rivers to the treetops, is full of life. Here are descriptions of four animals that make their home in the Amazon:

Green anaconda

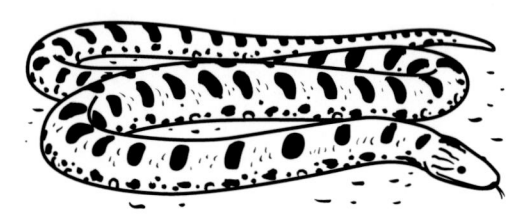

Green anacondas are the longest snakes in the world, reaching lengths of over 10 m. Anacondas are a type of boa constrictor. They usually ambush, or sneak up on, their prey from the water. When an animal such as a capybara or deer comes to drink, the anaconda quickly coils its body around the animal's neck and strangles it.

Capybara

Capybaras are the world's largest rodents. They can weigh up to 77 kg. Capybaras spend most of their time in groups around rivers and lakes, eating grasses and water plants. They are excellent swimmers and will enter the water to escape from predators. Capybaras have many enemies, including anacondas, caimans, jaguars and pumas.

Sloth

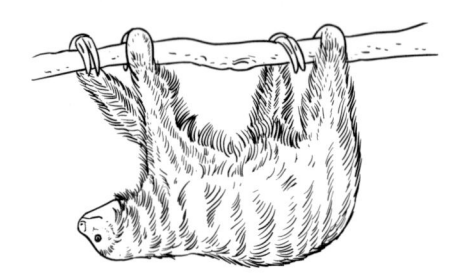

Sloths, which are about the size of a small to medium dog, have poor vision and hearing. They live in the canopy of the rainforest, spending most of their time hanging upside down by their large, hooked claws. Sloths eat leaves, fruit, buds and twigs. They move extremely slowly and only come down to the ground about once every six days. On the ground, sloths are completely helpless.

Piranha

Piranhas are small fish with razor-sharp teeth that live in the rivers of the Amazon Basin. Piranhas are known for quickly devouring much larger animals in a feeding frenzy. Although some piranhas will do this, they only prey on large animals when they are very hungry. Most of the time, they eat small fish and other small animals. Some species of piranha do not eat meat at all!

Name _____

Valuable resources

Amazon Rainforest wildlife

A. Answer the questions. Use the information on page 86 to help you.

1. How does an anaconda hunt and kill its prey?

   _____

2. Which animals prey on capybaras?

   _____

3. Why don't sloths come down to the ground very often?

   _____

4. What do piranhas eat?

   _____

B. Choose an animal from page 86 that you think is the most interesting. Draw a picture of it and then write a caption describing that animal.

Galápagos Islands wildlife

The Galápagos Islands, 966 km off the coast of Ecuador, are well-known for their unique wildlife. Many species that live on the islands are found nowhere else in the world. Almost all of the land and water are protected as part of a national park. Each year, more than 150 000 tourists visit the Galápagos, bringing in over $400 million to the economy of Ecuador. But increasing numbers of visitors can harm the environment. Scientists are working hard to strike a balance between what is good for the economy and what is good for nature.

Galápagos tortoise

Galápagos tortoises are the biggest tortoises in the world. Some can grow to be 1.2 m wide and up to 318 kg. They have a cooperative relationship with a small bird called the Galápagos finch. When the finch lands on the tortoise's shell, the tortoise will stretch out its neck to allow the bird to pick off ticks. Scientists believe there are 11 subspecies (kinds) of tortoises living on the different islands. Due to hunting in the past, there may be fewer than 5000 of these tortoises left. On one of the islands, a breeding programme is in place to try to restore the wild tortoise population.

Marine iguana

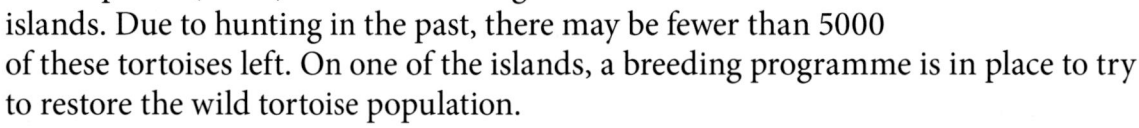

Marine iguanas can grow up to 1.2 m long. They are unusual because, unlike other iguanas, they swim and eat in the ocean. The marine iguana's diet consists of algae that grow on rocks in the shallow water near the shore. Marine iguanas can stay underwater for an entire hour while feeding. When they are not eating, they bask in the sun to warm their coldblooded bodies. Their enemies include rats that feast on iguana eggs and wild cats that hunt their young.

Galápagos penguin

Galápagos penguins are the only species of penguin that live near the equator. They keep cool by swimming in the cool ocean current during the day and returning to land at night when the air is cooler. At about only 46 cm tall, they are smaller than most other penguins. Galápagos penguins breed two or three times a year. The parents take turns caring for their eggs and the babies after they hatch. There are only about 2000 Galápagos penguins left, making them an endangered species.

Galápagos Islands wildlife

Read each clue below. Write the correct word on the numbered lines. Then use the numbers to crack the code!

1. There are only about 2000 Galápagos ___ left.

   ___ ___ ___ ___ ___ ___ ___ ___
   24   13   22   15   3   17   22   1

2. The marine iguana eats ___.

   ___ ___ ___ ___ ___
   9   20   15   9   13

3. The Galápagos tortoise and the Galápagos ___ have a cooperative relationship.

   ___ ___ ___ ___ ___
   14   17   22   11   16

4. The ___ must spend time basking in the sun to warm its body.

   ___ ___ ___ ___ ___ ___   ___ ___ ___ ___ ___ ___
   21   9   26   17   22   13   17   15   3   9   22   9

5. Galápagos penguins are the only penguins that live near the ___.

   ___ ___ ___ ___ ___ ___ ___
   13   25   3   9   2   23   26

6. The Galápagos ___ can weigh up to 318 kg.

   ___ ___ ___ ___ ___ ___ ___ ___
   2   23   26   2   23   17   1   13

Crack the code!

In 1972, the last known surviving Pinta Island tortoise (a subspecies of the Galápagos tortoise) was taken into captivity. Sadly, he died in 2012. His name was ___.

___ ___ ___ ___ ___ ___ ___ ___   ___ ___ ___ ___ ___ ___
20   23   22   13   1   23   21   13   15   13   23   26   15   13

Name _____

Valuable resources

Review

Use words from the box to complete the crossword puzzle.

alpacas
Brazil
capybara
Chile
Galápagos
Paraná
quinine
quinoa

Across

1. The ____ tortoise is the largest tortoise in the world.
5. ____ is a grain-like seed that grows in the Andes Mountains.
6. ____ exports more copper than any other country in the world.
7. About 200 million cows are raised in ____.

Down

2. The Itaipú Dam is on the ____ River.
3. ____ are raised for their soft, warm coats.
4. The ____ is the world's largest rodent.
5. ____ is used to treat malaria.

90 Exploring geography: South America   Prim-Ed Publishing www.prim-ed.com

South American culture

This section introduces pupils to the beliefs and traditions of the South American people. Pupils learn about cultural influences such as music, art and sports that are important parts of life in South America. They also learn about three famous tourist sites, as well as different types of South American cuisine and celebrations. Finally, pupils study the religions and indigenous cultures of South America.

CONTENTS

Overview 92–93	Indigenous cultures 104–105
Tourist attractions 94–95	South American cuisine 106–107
Arts and entertainment 96–101	Celebrations 108–109
Religions of South America 102–103	Review 110

Name _____

Culture

Overview

The culture of a group of people is reflected in its customs, traditions and beliefs. One way to learn about a particular culture is to explore its history, celebrations, art and religions. The culture of South America is a blend of traditions from indigenous groups, Spanish and other European settlers, and slaves from Africa who were brought to South America to work on plantations.

Tourist attractions

Thousands of people visit South America to see the ruins of the Inca city of Machu Picchu in Peru. People also travel to the isolated Easter Island, far off the coast of Chile, to see the mysterious stone sculptures of giant heads. In Rio de Janeiro, Brazil, the large statue of O Cristo Redentor (Christ the Redeemer) draws thousands of tourists each year.

Arts and entertainment

South America has a rich history of art, which includes the traditional artwork of the Incas. Popular dances such as the tango and samba began in South America. Important sports in South America include football and *capoeira* (cap-oh-AIR-ah), a type of martial art that incorporates music and dance.

Native cultures

Before the Spanish *conquistadors* (conquerors) came to South America, the land was inhabited by many indigenous people. One of the largest groups still in existence is the Quechua (KECH-wah) people in the Andes. Another group, the Yanomamo (yah-nuh-MAH-moh) in the Amazon Rainforest, have had little contact with the modern world and still live much as their ancestors did thousands of years ago. The Mapuche (mah-POO-chay), who live in Argentina and Chile, were never conquered by the Incas or Spanish, so they have held on to their own culture.

Cuisine

South American cuisine is influenced by Europeans and Africans who have come to South America, as well as by traditional dishes of the indigenous people. Stews and soups are popular in almost every region. People in South America also enjoy a wide variety of locally grown fruits and vegetables.

Religions and celebrations

About 85% of the people in South America are Roman Catholic. Some of the most celebrated holidays are religious, including Christmas and Easter. Carnaval is a holiday that is celebrated just before the start of *lent,* a 40-day holy period before Easter. Music, dancing and traditional foods are an important part of the Carnaval celebration.

Name _____

Culture

Overview

Tick the correct box to answer each question.

1. Which of these are the ruins of an Inca city?
   ☐ Rio de Janeiro
   ☐ Quechua
   ☐ Machu Picchu
   ☐ O Cristo Redentor

2. What is *capoeira*?
   ☐ a kind of martial art
   ☐ a group of people who live in the Amazon Rainforest
   ☐ a holiday that is celebrated before lent
   ☐ a popular dance

3. Where do the Yanomamo live?
   ☐ in the Andes
   ☐ at Machu Picchu
   ☐ on Easter Island
   ☐ in the Amazon Rainforest

4. Which of these foods are popular throughout South America?
   ☐ ham and eggs
   ☐ soups and stews
   ☐ pasta and meatballs
   ☐ pizza and salad

5. About what percentage of the population of South America is Roman Catholic?
   ☐ 80%
   ☐ 85%
   ☐ 90%
   ☐ 95%

Name _____

Culture

Tourist attractions

There are many interesting landmarks to visit in South America. Each year, these sites attract hundreds of thousands of tourists who want to learn more about South America's history and culture.

Machu Picchu

Nestled in the Andes Mountains of Peru lies Machu Picchu, the remains of an ancient Inca city. The Incas were the indigenous people of South America who once ruled much of the west coast. Archaeologists believe the city, which was built in the 1400s, was made for royalty. Machu Picchu is built of stone blocks and includes palaces, temples, storehouses and tombs. There are also courtyards, plazas, fountains, and over 100 flights of stairs. The city was abandoned just over 100 years after it was built, around the same time Spanish conquistadors began invading South America. However, it appears that the Spanish never found the city itself, because they did not destroy any of its buildings the way they did at other Inca sites.

O Cristo Redentor

At the peak of Corcovado Mountain, high above the city of Rio de Janeiro in Brazil, stands the 40 m statue of O Cristo Redentor (Christ the Redeemer). This giant statue of Jesus is made from concrete and soapstone and can be seen throughout the city. The statue was completed in 1931. It is a popular destination for tourists who are willing to climb the 220 steps to reach it!

Easter Island

Easter Island is an isolated island located in the Pacific Ocean nearly 4023 km from Chile. Although the people who once lived on Easter Island are gone, they left behind hundreds of large stone statues of human heads and torsos called *moai* (MOH-eye). These statues, which were likely carved between 1100 and 1680, weigh about 13 tonnes each. It remains a mystery how they were moved from the place where they were carved to their locations around the island.

Culture

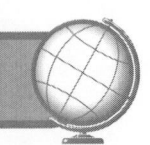

Tourist attractions

A. Unscramble the word or words under each line to complete the sentence.

Some answers will need to start with capital letters.

1. O Cristo Redentor is made from _____ and soapstone.
   rocceent

2. Machu Picchu was built by the _____
   nasci

3. There are hundreds of statues of human heads on _____.
   trease dialns

4. Easter Island is located in the _____.
   faccipi necao

5. Archaeologists think Machu Picchu was built for Inca _____.
   yarotyl

6. O Cristo Redentor is located on _____.
   vacoocrod tunimona

7. _____ is located in the Andes Mountains.
   humca hucpic

8. Machu Picchu was likely abandoned because of Spanish _____.
   qoncsudatosri

9. No one knows how the _____ giant stone heads of Easter Island were moved.
   mrysseoiut

B. Which of the three places on the other page would you most like to visit? Explain your answer.

_____

_____

_____

Name _____

Arts and entertainment

Inca arts

The Inca empire once stretched along South America's west coast, from the northern border of modern Ecuador to the middle of Chile. The Incas had a practical view of art. The arts they created had a function in everyday life.

Architecture

The Incas were master stone builders. Buildings were made with huge stones that were carved to fit together perfectly. In fact, the stones fit so tightly that not even a thin knife could be squeezed between them. This made the buildings very stable in the frequent earthquakes that occurred in that area. The stones that the Incas used sometimes weighed up to several tonnes and often had to be moved some distance to the construction site. No one is really sure how they did that. They may have used a system of logs and ramps similar to those used by the Egyptians to build the pyramids.

The Incas also used stone to build step-like terraces on the steep mountainsides. The terraces made flat areas for growing crops and kept the soil from washing down the hills when it rained.

Pottery

The Incas did not make their pots on a turning wheel. Instead, they shaped them by hand or used moulds. They decorated their pots with pictures of animals, such as birds, fish, butterflies and llamas, as well as flowers and peppers. They also used patterns of squares, diamonds, triangles or other geometric shapes. Each village or region was often known for a specific pattern. The Incas usually painted their pots in red, black, yellow or white.

Metalwork

The Incas also made many objects from gold and silver. However, very few Inca metal pieces survived. When the Spanish invaded Inca lands in the 1500s, the conquistadors took many of these items. Rather than valuing the metalwork as art, the Spanish melted it down to make coins, which were then shipped back to Spain.

Name _____

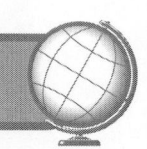

Culture

Arts and entertainment

Inca arts

A. Use the information on page 96 to complete the sentences.

1. The Incas' main building material was _____.

2. Inca buildings were strong enough to withstand _____.

3. The Incas may have moved stones in much the same way as the _____ did.

4. Incas built stone _____ for mountainside farming.

5. Inca pots were decorated with _____ shapes.

6. Inca villages were often known for using specific _____ to decorate their pottery.

7. Very few pieces of Inca _____ survived the Spanish invasion.

B. Use the information on the other page to help you create a design for the Inca pot. Colour your design with traditional Inca colours.

Name _____

Culture

Arts and entertainment

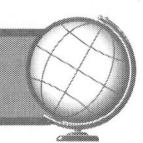

Music and dance

Different South American regions are known for their own kinds of music and dance. Musicians and dancers often wear elaborate and colourful outfits.

Huayño

Huayño is a type of music and dance that originated in the Andes Mountains in Peru. Musicians play a variety of instruments, including the violin, charango (a small guitar), quena (a kind of flute), siku (a pan flute) and harp. Huayño is danced by both couples and groups and involves complicated turns, hops and toe taps. Audience members clap, whistle and sing the words to the songs, which are often in Quechua, the Peruvian native language.

Tango

The tango is a dramatic, romantic ballroom dance performed by couples. It originated in Buenos Aires, Argentina, where it became popular in the early and mid 1900s. Dance halls throughout the city were filled every night with men and women dancing the tango. Eventually, the dance spread to Europe and North America. Today, the tango is one of the most popular ballroom dances in the world.

Samba

Samba is a type of music and dance that was brought to Brazil by African slaves who worked on plantations. Over the years, samba spread to the entire Brazilian culture. There are many variations of samba dance, but all are lively with a strong rhythm. The dance features fast footwork and rapid movements. Percussion instruments such as drums and shakers are an important part of samba music. The samba is a big part of the yearly Carnaval celebration, where thousands of costumed dancers perform. Rio de Janeiro has over 70 samba groups that compete for prizes during Carnaval.

98   Exploring geography: South America   Prim-Ed Publishing   www.prim-ed.com

Name _____

Culture

Arts and entertainment

Music and dance

Circle the correct word or words to complete each sentence. Use information from page 98 to help you.

1. The tango is performed by ____.

   groups   **couples**   **acrobats**

2. Huayño music and dance come from ____.

   Brazil   **Argentina**   **Peru**

3. The tango came from Buenos Aires in the country of ____.

   Brazil   **Argentina**   **Peru**

4. African slaves brought samba dance and music to the country of ____.

   Brazil   **Argentina**   **Peru**

5. A charango is a ____.

   small guitar   **lively dance**   **yearly celebration**

6. ____ is an important part of Carnaval.

   Huayño   **Tango**   **Samba**

7. Many huayño songs are sung in ____.

   Spanish   **Portuguese**   **Quechua**

8. The ____ is one of the most popular ballroom dances in the world.

   samba   **tango**   **huayño**

9. ____ involves hops, turns and toe taps.

   Huayño   **Tango**   **Samba**

10. The ____ features drums, shakers and other percussion instruments.

    tango   **huayño**   **samba**

Name _____

Culture

Arts and entertainment

Sports

People in South America enjoy participating in and attending many sporting events. Popular sports include football, rugby, baseball, horse racing, motor racing and capoeira, an unusual form of martial art.

Football

Football is by far the most popular sport in South America. Football first came to South America when British sailors played the game in Argentina. The sport soon spread to the local population and across the continent. The very first international football championship, the World Cup, was held in Uruguay in 1930. Uruguay and Argentina took first and second place, respectively.

Although people across the continent enjoy football, Brazilians are especially wild about the sport. Brazil has won the World Cup five times—more than any other country. The World Cup was held in Brazil in 1950 and is scheduled to be there again in 2014.

Brazil is home to perhaps the greatest football player of all time: Pelé. Known for his kicking power and accuracy, Pelé won his first World Cup in 1958 when he was 17 years old. Pelé is the all-time leading scorer for the Brazilian national team. He is the only football player to be part of three World Cup-winning teams.

Capoeira

Capoeira is a form of martial art that incorporates acrobatics, dance and music. The sport originated in Brazil with African slaves who wanted to defend themselves against their owners. Because slaves were forbidden to practise self-defence, they cleverly set the movements to music, making it look like a dance.

Capoeira involves two athletes who do a series of spins, somersaults, flips and kicks. They often come very close to each other, but do not actually make contact. In capoeira, speed and cunning are valued over strength. The movements are done in time to the music of drums, tambourines, and a single-stringed African instrument called a *berimbau* (buh-REEM-bow).

Even after slavery was abolished in 1888, capoeira was forbidden. It did not become legal until 1937. Today, capoeira is a respected sport, both in South America and in other parts of the world.

Arts and entertainment

Sports

A. Read each statement. Circle **yes** if it is true or **no** if it is false. Use the information on page 100 to help you.

1. Rugby is the most popular sport in South America.   Yes   No
2. The first football players in Argentina were Spanish.   Yes   No
3. The first football World Cup was held in Uruguay in 1930.   Yes   No
4. Brazil won the first World Cup Championship.   Yes   No
5. Brazil has won the World Cup five times.   Yes   No
6. Brazil hosted the World Cup in 1950.   Yes   No
7. Pelé is a great football player from Uruguay.   Yes   No
8. Capoeira is a kind of martial art that began in Brazil.   Yes   No
9. People who are doing capoeira look like they are dancing.   Yes   No
10. A berimbau is a type of drum from Africa.   Yes   No
11. In the sport of capoeira, it is very important to be strong.   Yes   No
12. Capoeira was made legal in 1888.   Yes   No

B. Why was capoeira set to music and made to look like a dance?

_____

_____

Name _____

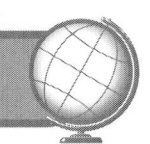

Culture

Religions of South America

Before the arrival of the Spanish conquistadors in the early 1500s, most indigenous cultures in South America practised *shamanism*. In shamanism, people called shamans were thought to have the power to heal and to communicate with the supernatural. Shamans had rituals to celebrate various events and individual accomplishments, such as the change of seasons or a boy becoming a man.

When the Spanish conquistadors arrived, they brought many Roman Catholic missionaries to South America. These missionaries converted most of the indigenous people to Catholicism and outlawed all indigenous religions. Some traditional beliefs and customs were wiped out completely, and others were mixed with those of the Catholic religion. Today, about 85% of the population in South America is Roman Catholic.

Catholic church in Brazil

Another religion that came to South America from overseas is Candomblé. Candomblé is a mix of several African religions that were brought to Brazil by slaves. Over time, South Americans blended these beliefs with some aspects of Catholicism. People who practise Candomblé believe in one all-powerful god who is served by smaller gods. About 2 million people, mostly in Brazil, are followers of Candomblé.

There are also small populations of other religions in South America. For example, about 28 000 Mennonites live in Paraguay. Several Jewish communities thrive in the cities of Buenos Aires, São Paulo and Rio de Janeiro.

A. What happened to the indigenous religions of South America when the Spanish arrived?

_____

_____

_____

Name _____

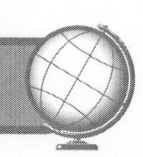

Culture

Religions of South America

B. Read each clue below. Write the correct word on the numbered lines. Then use the numbers to crack the code!

1. Before the Spanish conquistadors came, most indigenous cultures practised ___.

   $\overline{17}\ \overline{2}\ \overline{9}\ \overline{23}\ \overline{9}\ \overline{22}\ \overline{1}\ \overline{17}\ \overline{23}$

2. About 28 000 Mennonites live in ___.

   $\overline{20}\ \overline{9}\ \overline{18}\ \overline{9}\ \overline{3}\ \overline{15}\ \overline{9}\ \overline{11}$

3. Spanish ___ converted most of the South American population to Catholicism.

   $\overline{23}\ \overline{1}\ \overline{17}\ \overline{17}\ \overline{1}\ \overline{21}\ \overline{22}\ \overline{9}\ \overline{18}\ \overline{1}\ \overline{5}\ \overline{17}$

4. ___ is a mix of several different African religions.

   $\overline{7}\ \overline{9}\ \overline{22}\ \overline{6}\ \overline{21}\ \overline{23}\ \overline{8}\ \overline{24}\ \overline{5}$

5. Today, about 85% of the South American population is ___.

   $\overline{18}\ \overline{21}\ \overline{23}\ \overline{9}\ \overline{22}$ $\overline{7}\ \overline{9}\ \overline{16}\ \overline{2}\ \overline{21}\ \overline{24}\ \overline{1}\ \overline{7}$

6. Candomblé was brought to ___ by African slaves.

   $\overline{8}\ \overline{18}\ \overline{9}\ \overline{10}\ \overline{1}\ \overline{24}$

Crack the code!

This religion is growing in South America today.

$\overline{20}\ \overline{18}\ \overline{21}\ \overline{16}\ \overline{5}\ \overline{17}\ \overline{16}\ \overline{9}\ \overline{22}\ \overline{16}\ \overline{1}\ \overline{17}\ \overline{23}$

Indigenous cultures

The Quechua

The Quechua people have lived in the Andes Mountains for thousands of years. Although much of their culture has been changed by the Incas and the Spanish, they still speak the Quechua language and practise many of their old traditions. One such tradition comes from the Quechua word *ayni*, which means 'to help one another'. The practice of *ayni* has helped the Quechua survive in the harsh environment of the Andes.

The Quechua depend on llamas and alpacas for many of their daily needs, including meat, wool, fertiliser and leather. The Quechua also use llamas as pack animals when travelling through the mountains. Girls who tend to the llamas are called *llameras*. There are special songs and dances that llameras perform while taking care of the llamas. These dances are also performed at major festivals.

The Mapuche

The Mapuche live in south-central Chile and Argentina. Unlike other South American cultures, the Mapuche were never conquered by the Incas or the Spanish. They fought hard to hold on to their culture and their land, resisting the Spanish missionaries and going to war against the conquistadors.

However, the Mapuche still lost a great deal of their land to Chile after the country gained independence from Spain in the 1800s. To the Mapuche, whose name means 'people of the land', the land is sacred. Today, the Mapuche still speak their native language, Mapuzugun. Most make their living as farmers, and they often work together as a community during harvest time.

The Yanomamo

The Yanomamo live deep in the rainforests of Brazil and Venezuela. Until recently, they have had very little contact with the outside world. Many Yanomamo still live as their ancestors did for thousands of years. They have no written language and depend on the rainforest for everything they need. People live together in structures made from tree trunks, vines and leaves. They make their own baskets, hammocks, tools and weapons. They grow some food in gardens but depend mostly on hunting animals and gathering wild fruits. Food is so abundant in the rainforest that the Yanomamo need only work about three hours a day to survive.

The Yanomamo have a history of warfare, and tribes are frequently at war with one another. About one-third of Yanomamo men die in battle. However, the biggest threat to the Yanomamo today are outsiders who want to take their land. Outsiders have also brought deadly diseases such as malaria to the people.

Name _____

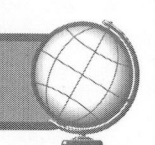

Indigenous cultures

Write two interesting facts about the Quechua, Mapuche and Yanomamo cultures. Use the information on page 104 to help you.

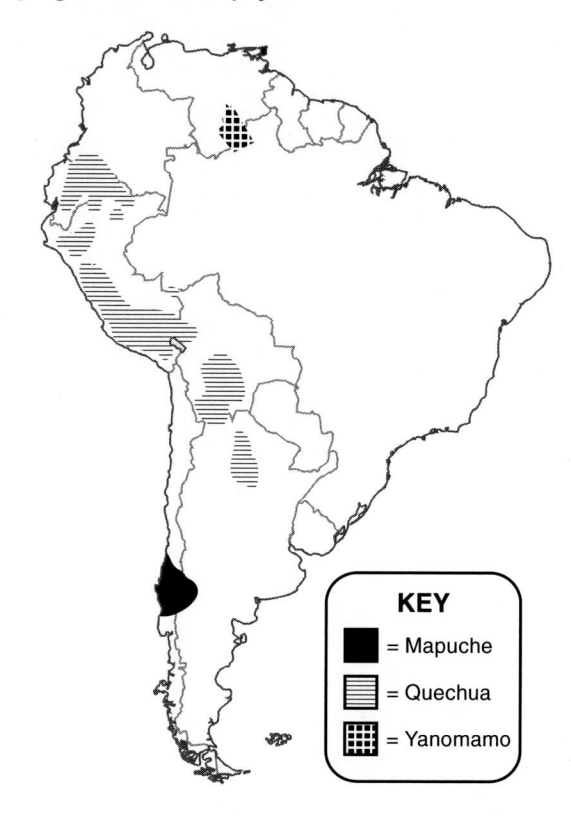

KEY
■ = Mapuche
☰ = Quechua
▦ = Yanomamo

Quechua

1. _____

2. _____

Mapuche

1. _____

2. _____

Yanomamo

1. _____

2. _____

South American cuisine

The cuisine of South America is a tasty blend of indigenous foods, African dishes and European recipes brought over from Spain, Portugal and Italy.

Different regions of South America specialise in different cuisines. Near the coast, seafood is popular. Communities that live near the rainforest have a great deal of fruit in their diets. In the Andes Mountains, potatoes are eaten with every meal. In fact, over 100 different kinds of potatoes are grown in the Andes. In Argentina and Brazil, grilled beef is served frequently. Here are some other dishes that are popular in South America:

Empanadas

Empanadas are crescent-shaped pastries made from wheat or corn flour. They are filled with meats and cheeses and then baked or fried. Empanadas are usually served with salsa. Although they are eaten throughout South America, different regions prepare them in different ways. They can be found at roadside stands, as well as on the menus of fancy restaurants.

empanadas

Stews and soups

People enjoy stews and soups in many parts of South America. The national dish of Brazil is *feijoada completa,* which is a stew of black beans, smoked meats and sausage. In Colombia, people eat *sancocho,* a stew of meat, corn and other vegetables. Fish soups are popular in Chile, and people in Paraguay eat a beef and dumpling stew called *bori-bori*. In the northern countries of Guyana and Suriname, people eat a stew called pepper pot, made with cassava juice, meat and hot peppers.

sancocho

Mate tea

Mate (MAH-tay) is a kind of tea that is popular throughout South America, especially in Argentina, Uruguay, Paraguay, Chile and Brazil. It comes from the yerba mate plant, which is a type of holly. Mate is brewed in a small gourd and drunk through a metal straw. It is usually shared among family and friends. Although the taste is bitter, it is thought to have many health benefits.

mate

South American cuisine

For each type of food, write the letter of the clue that matches it. Then find the nine kinds of food in the word search. Words may appear across, down, or diagonally.

_____ 1. sancocho

_____ 2. empanada

_____ 3. mate

_____ 4. feijoada completa

_____ 5. potatoes

_____ 6. fish soup

_____ 7. fruit

_____ 8. pepper pot

_____ 9. beef

a. a popular dish in Chile

b. served grilled in Brazil and Argentina

c. a stew made with cassava juice

d. a large part of the diet of people who live near the rainforest

e. the national dish of Brazil

f. a stew eaten in Colombia

g. a food commonly eaten in the Andes Mountains

h. a crescent-shaped pastry

i. a tea that is drunk through a metal straw

```
M Y B P X H S A N D I D I G O L
Y O U E R F I S H S O U P L I L
F E B P E L O L G O O E D R T C
H I N P F F U A D J E O A Y D A
B L S E S R I F N B S C E T A B
U A N R Y D U Y O U H R M F V F
A P M P I U Y I I E N D P L I E
G O H O R T B E T N I C A E D Z
O T E T S A N C O C H O N A S G
O A Y T H R E A E T L O A T S X
O T C H O C O E T A T D D E I T
C O E C R E T T A W A E A A R W
F E I J O A D A C O M P L E T A
N S O T M K M N E P Q U A N K O
```

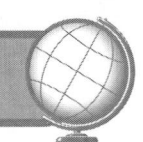

Celebrations

Carnaval

Throughout South America, Carnaval is celebrated before lent, a 40-day holy period for Catholics that ends on Easter Sunday. Carnaval is a time for people to have fun. The celebration usually starts on a Friday in February and runs until the following Tuesday. During Carnaval, people dress up in colourful costumes. There is plenty to eat and drink at huge parades and block parties, called *blacos,* where people dance in the streets.

The largest Carnaval celebration in the world takes place in Rio de Janeiro, Brazil. In Brazil, most people get the entire week off as a holiday. The streets are alive day and night with music and dancing. Carnaval in Rio de Janeiro ends with the samba parade. Samba groups from all over the region work all year long building floats, designing costumes, creating music and practicing dances for the parade.

Answer the questions using the information above.

1. In which month does Carnaval usually start? _____

2. What is the name of the holy 40-day period that follows Carnaval? _____

3. Where is the biggest Carnaval celebration held? _____

4. What are two things that people do during Carnaval?

   _____

5. Why do people celebrate Carnaval?

   _____

   _____

6. How do people prepare for the samba parade?

   _____

   _____

Name _____

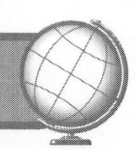

Culture

Celebrations

Christmas traditions

Most South American families celebrate Christmas Eve by attending at least one church service and having a large dinner. Songs are sung and gifts are exchanged. Families display a nativity (manger) scene, which serves as the centre of activities. People decorate their homes with fresh flowers and attend fireworks displays on Christmas Eve. Sometimes people go to the beach on Christmas Day.

Country	Tradition
Argentina	On Christmas Eve, people light large paper balloons that take off into the night sky. Children receive their gifts on Three Kings Day, which is January 6.
Brazil	Brazilian children get gifts from Papai Noel (Father Christmas). Brazilians say that Papai Noel lives in Greenland and wears clothing made of silk.
Colombia	Starting on 16 December, the nine days of the Novena are observed. Each night, families attend at least one church service and sing and pray together. Colombians say that presents are brought by the Baby Jesus.
Ecuador	Children write notes to the Baby Jesus and put them in their shoes. They leave the shoes on the windowsills on Christmas Eve. On Christmas morning, the shoes are filled with noise-making toys.
Venezuela	Streets are closed to cars so that people can rollerskate to early morning church services. The night before Three Kings Day, children leave straw out. Venezuelans say that the Kings' horses eat the straw during the night and the Kings leave gifts and sweets.

Circle the correct answer.

1. Most families go to ___ on Christmas Eve. **a parade** **church**
2. The ___ is the centre of activities. **nativity** **Christmas tree**
3. On Christmas Day, people may ___. **play in the snow** **go to the beach**
4. In ___, children leave notes in their shoes. **Argentina** **Ecuador**
5. In Venezuela, people go to church on ___. **horses** **rollerskates**
6. Brazilians say that Papai Noel lives in ___. **Greenland** **the North Pole**
7. Children put ___ out on Three Kings Eve. **straw** **cookies**
8. Large paper balloons are lit in ___. **Colombia** **Argentina**

Name _____

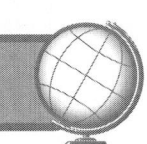

Culture

Review

Use words from the box to complete the crossword puzzle.

Argentina
Carnaval
empanada
Incas
Machu Picchu
missionaries
Pelé
Quechua

Across

2. ____ converted native South Americans to Catholicism.
4. The tango originated in ____.
6. a champion football player from Brazil
8. an ancient Inca city

Down

1. a holiday just before lent
3. The ____ are known for their stone-building skills and pottery.
5. a crescent-shaped pastry
7. The ____ are indigenous people who live in the Andes Mountains.

SECTION 6

Assessment

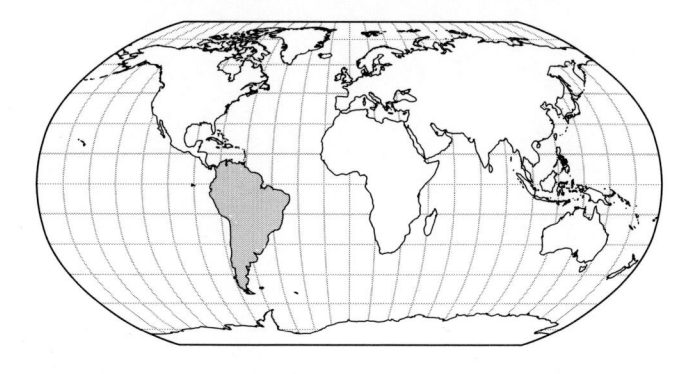

This section provides two cumulative assessments that you can use to evaluate pupils' acquisition of the information presented in this book. The first assessment requires pupils to identify selected cities, countries, landforms and bodies of water on a combined physical and political map. The second assessment is a two-page multiple-choice test covering information from all sections of the book. Use one or both assessments as culminating activities for your class's study of South America.

CONTENTS

Map test 112   Multiple-choice test 113–114

Name _____

Assessment

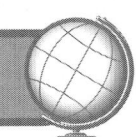

Map test

Write the name of the country, city, landform or ocean that matches each number. Use the words in the box to help you.

| Andes Mountains | Pacific Ocean | Atlantic Ocean | Falkland Islands | Uruguay |
| Tierra del Fuego | Buenos Aires | Colombia | Atacama Desert | Brazil |

1. _____
2. _____
3. _____
4. _____
5. _____
6. _____
7. _____
8. _____
9. _____
10. _____

Exploring geography: South America

Name _____

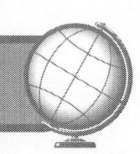

Multiple-choice test

Tick the correct box to answer each question or complete each sentence.

1. South America is the ____-largest continent in size.
   ☐ second
   ☐ third
   ☐ fourth
   ☐ fifth

2. Which ocean is west of South America?
   ☐ Atlantic
   ☐ Arctic
   ☐ Pacific
   ☐ Indian

3. In which two hemispheres is most of South America located?
   ☐ Northern and Southern
   ☐ Southern and Western
   ☐ Eastern and Western
   ☐ Northern and Western

4. Which of these is *not* a country in South America?
   ☐ Suriname
   ☐ Bolivia
   ☐ Argentina
   ☐ Mexico

5. The Andes Mountains run through the country of ____.
   ☐ Brazil
   ☐ Uruguay
   ☐ Bolivia
   ☐ Guyana

6. About 20% of the world's ____ is produced in the Amazon Rainforest.
   ☐ water
   ☐ oxygen
   ☐ lumber
   ☐ fruit

7. Which of these is *not* a river in South America?
   ☐ Amazon
   ☐ Orinoco
   ☐ Paraguay
   ☐ Nile

8. What is the name of the driest desert on Earth?
   ☐ Atacama
   ☐ Titicaca
   ☐ Gran Chaco
   ☐ Tierra del Fuego

Name _____

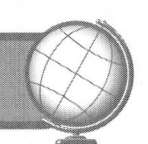

Multiple-choice test

9. In which country are the largest deposits of oil located?
   - ☐ Colombia
   - ☐ Ecuador
   - ☐ Venezuela
   - ☐ Peru

10. Chile supplies about 30% of the world's ____.
    - ☐ copper
    - ☐ tin
    - ☐ silver
    - ☐ zinc

11. Where do most Brazil nuts come from?
    - ☐ orchards in Brazil
    - ☐ the Andes Mountains
    - ☐ the Amazon Rainforest
    - ☐ the Pampas

12. Which statement is *not* true?
    - ☐ Llamas are bigger than alpacas.
    - ☐ Llamas are wild animals.
    - ☐ Llamas are used as pack animals.
    - ☐ Llamas may spit when angry.

13. In the 1900s, the tango became popular in ____.
    - ☐ Argentina
    - ☐ Brazil
    - ☐ Peru
    - ☐ Paraguay

14. The prominent religion in South America is ____.
    - ☐ Protestantism
    - ☐ Catholicism
    - ☐ Judaism
    - ☐ Mennonite

15. Who built Machu Picchu?
    - ☐ the Mapuche
    - ☐ Spanish missionaries
    - ☐ the Yanomamo
    - ☐ the Incas

16. Where is the biggest Carnaval celebration held?
    - ☐ Rio de Janeiro
    - ☐ Buenos Aires
    - ☐ Lima
    - ☐ São Paulo

Note-takers

This section provides four note-taker forms that give pupils the opportunity to culminate their study of South America by doing independent research on places or animals of their choice. (Some suggested topics are given below.) Pupils may use printed reference materials or internet sites to gather information on their topics. A cover page is also provided so that pupils may create a booklet of note-takers and any other reproducible pages from the book that you would like pupils to save.

FORMS

Physical feature 116

Suggested topics:
- Iguazu Falls
- Lake Maracaibo
- Los Glaciares National Park
- Pantanal
- São Francisco River

Animal 117

Suggested topics:
- Andean condor
- Blue-footed booby
- Howler monkey
- Jaguar
- Maned wolf

Tourist attraction 118

Suggested topics:
- Castillo de San Felipe de Barajas (Colombia)
- Inca Trail (Peru)
- Nazca Lines (Peru)
- Ollantaytambo (Peru)
- Sambadrome (Brazil)

City 119

Suggested topics:
- Brasília, Brazil
- Buenos Aires, Argentina
- Cuzco, Peru
- Mendoza, Argentina
- Quito, Ecuador

Cover page 120

Name _____

Physical feature

Select a physical feature of South America. Write notes about it to complete each section.

_____
(Name of physical feature)

Location

Interesting facts

Description

Animals or plants

Name _____

Animal

Draw a South American animal. Write notes about it to complete each section.

_____
(Name of animal)

Endangered? Yes No

Physical characteristics

Habitat

Diet

Behaviours

Enemies/defences

Name _____

Tourist attraction

Draw a South American tourist attraction. Then write notes about it to complete each section.

_____
(Name of tourist attraction)

Location

Description

Interesting facts

118 Exploring geography: South America   Prim-Ed Publishing www.prim-ed.com

Name _____

City

Select a South American city you would like to visit. Write notes about it to complete each section.

My trip to _____
(Name of city)

Location

_____
_____
_____
_____

How I would get there

_____
_____
_____
_____

Things I would see and do

_____
_____
_____
_____
_____
_____
_____

Foods I would eat

_____
_____
_____
_____

Learning the language

How to say 'hello':

_____

How to say 'goodbye':

_____

www.prim-ed.com   Prim-Ed Publishing   Exploring geography: South America   **119**

SOUTH AMERICA

Answers

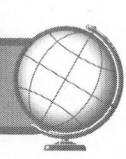

Page 7

1. fourth-largest continent
2. North America
3. Pacific and Atlantic oceans
4. South America is located mostly in both the Southern and Western hemispheres.
5. describes a place by using another place it is near

Page 8

A. Africa, south, Antarctica, Pacific, east

B. Pupils should colour North America orange and Africa yellow, and circle the Atlantic Ocean in blue. They should draw a penguin on Antarctica.

Page 11

A. 1. c 2. f 3. h 4. e 5. d 6. b 7. g 8. i 9. a

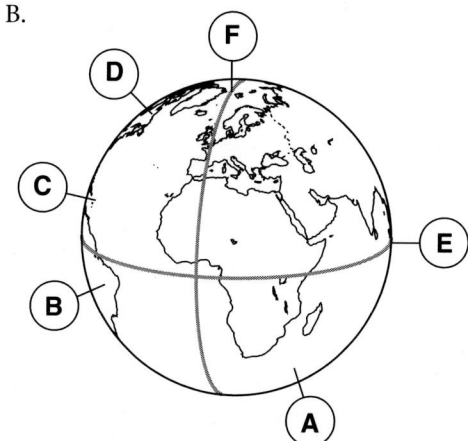

B.

Page 13

A.
1. equator
2. prime meridian
3. south
4. 60 °W
5. 90 °S
6. latitude lines
7. 15 degrees
8. 20 °N
9. 80 °W

B. because most places in South America are south of the equator and west of the prime meridian

Page 14

A.
1. No
2. Yes
3. Yes
4. No
5. Yes
6. No
7. Yes
8. Yes

B. three: North America, South America and Antarctica

Page 16

Across
2. Atlantic
3. hemispheres
6. Africa
8. projection

Down
1. Pacific
4. relative
5. equator
7. fourth

Page 19

1. fourth
2. 12
3. Brazil
4. near the coast
5. Cairo

Page 20

A. Pupils should colour each bar a different colour, then complete the caption. Answers will vary.

Page 21

B.
1. tripled
2. faster than
3. 112
4. 300
5. 458
6. 1970
7. 2050

C. Answers will vary. Teacher check.

Page 23

A. Pupils should colour Bolivia, Chile, Ecuador and Peru yellow. They should colour Colombia, Guyana, Suriname, Venezuela and French Guiana green. They should also colour Argentina, Brazil, Paraguay, Uruguay and the Falkland Islands red.

B.
1. No
2. Yes
3. No
4. No
5. Yes
6. Yes
7. No
8. Yes
9. No

Page 24

A. Answers will vary. Teacher check.

Answers

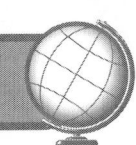

Page 25

B. Pupils should colour each country a different colour.

Country	Colour
1. Brazil	Colour will vary.
2. Argentina	Colour will vary.
3. Peru	Colour will vary.
4. Colombia	Colour will vary.
5. Bolivia	Colour will vary.

Page 26

A. Pupils should colour each bar a different colour.

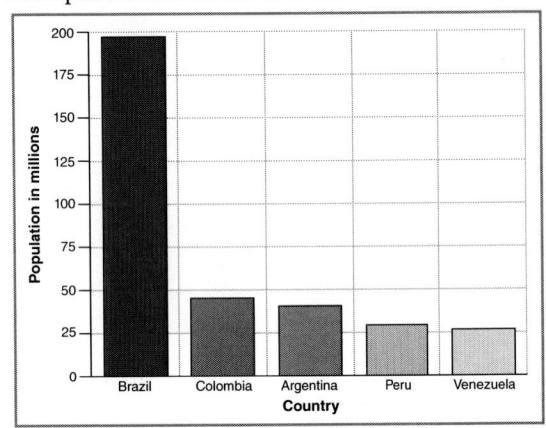

Page 27

B.
1. 6
2. Colombia
3. Argentina, Colombia
4. Peru
5. Venezuela
6. Brazil

C. Answers will vary. Teacher check.

Page 28

B.
1. Yes
2. No
3. Yes
4. No
5. No
6. Yes
7. No
8. No

Page 29

A. Pupils should label each country and then colour it a different colour. Captions will vary. Teacher check.

Page 30

A.
1. Lima
2. Santiago
3. Guayaquil
4. Quito
5. Santa Cruz
6. La Paz

Page 31

B. Peru, Andes, cities, Lima

C.
1. e
2. c
3. f
4. h
5. j
6. a
7. g
8. d
9. i
10. b

Answers

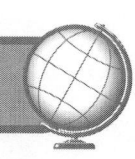

Page 32

B. 1. four
   2. Venezuela
   3. Colombia
   4. Suriname
   5. French Guiana
   6. Guyana
   7. because it has many rivers

Page 33

A. Pupils should label each country and dependency and then colour each of them a different colour. Captions will vary. Teacher check.

Page 35

1. Venezuela
2. Bogotá
3. Colombia
4. Guyana
5. Maracaibo
6. Mestizo
7. ranked

Crack the code!
The world's largest supply of <u>emeralds</u> comes from Colombia.

Page 36

B. 1. dependency
   2. Brazil
   3. Argentina
   4. Paraguay
   5. Uruguay
   6. Argentina
   7. Atlantic Ocean
   8. west

Page 37

A. Pupils should label each country and dependency and then colour each of them a different colour. Captions will vary. Teacher check.

Page 39

A. 1. Brasília, Brazil
   2. Belém, Brazil
   3. Buenos Aires, Argentina
   4. Rosario, Argentina

B. 1. Montevideo   6. 1 160 000
   2. Fortaleza   7. Brasília
   3. three   8. São Paulo
   4. Brazil   9. Campinas
   5. Córdoba   10. Fortaleza

Answers

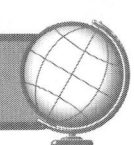

Page 40

1. Caracas
2. Georgetown
3. Paramaribo
4. Bogotá
5. Quito
6. Lima
7. La Paz
8. Brasília
9. Asunción
10. Santiago
11. Buenos Aires
12. Montevideo

Pupils should colour Argentina, Chile, Colombia, Guyana, Paraguay, Peru, Suriname, Uruguay and Venezuela. Teacher check.

Page 42

Across
3. Buenos Aires
5. coast
6. Chile
7. Andes

Down
1. fourth
2. Brazil
4. Caracas
5. Colombia

Page 45

1. Southern Tundra
2. Mount Aconcagua
3. Patagonia
4. second
5. South America is bordered only by the Atlantic Ocean and Caribbean Sea.

Page 46

A.
1. Andes Mountains
2. Atacama Desert
3. Mount Aconcagua
4. Brazilian Highlands
5. Guiana Highlands
6. Falkland Islands
7. Patagonia
8. northern

B. Pupils should colour the Andes Mountains brown and the Atacama Desert yellow. They should also circle the three highlands in orange and the Amazon Basin in green. Teacher check.

Page 49

1. 8851 km
2. Aconcagua
3. Huascarán
4. chinchilla
5. Pissis
6. condor
7. vicuña
8. Ojos del Salado
9. Nazca
10. Ring of Fire

Page 51

A.
1. Guiana
2. Brazilian
3. Patagonia
4. Brazilian
5. Guiana
6. Brazilian
7. Patagonia

B.
1. A sandstone plateau with steep cliffs, also known as a tableland.
2. house of the gods
3. erosion by the Amazon River
4. Argentina and Chile

Page 53

A.
1. the Pampas
2. Llanos
3. the Pampas
4. Gran Chaco
5. Llanos
6. Gran Chaco
7. Gran Chaco
8. the Pampas
9. Llanos

B.
1. A large, mostly flat area of land that usually has few or no trees.
2. A level area of land that is low in elevation.

Page 55

A.
1. third
2. emergent
3. oxygen
4. insects
5. canopy
6. anacondas

B. emergent, canopy, understorey, forest floor

Page 57

A. Andes, driest, rain/rainfall, fog, underground, volcanic, copper

B. Answers will vary. Teacher check.

Page 58

A.
1. Yes
2. No
3. No
4. Yes
5. Yes
6. No
7. Yes
8. Yes
9. Yes

Page 59

B. Pupils should trace the dotted line between Chile and Argentina in red and trace the route through the Strait of Magellan in blue. Then they should label the map. Teacher check.

C. Ferdinand Magellan saw all the fires the indigenous Indians had built to keep warm, so he named the area 'land of fire'.

Answers

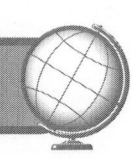

Page 60

A. 1. west
2. Magellan
3. Amazon
4. São Francisco
5. Titicaca
6. Venezuela

Page 61

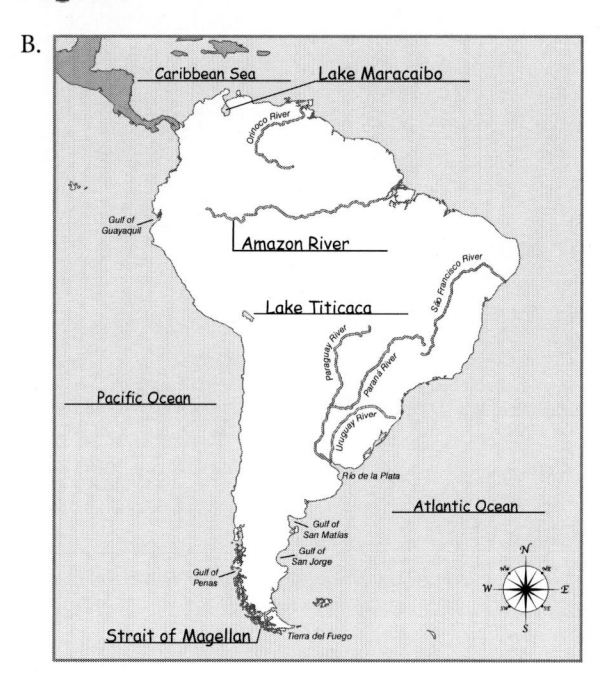

B. [Map of South America with labels: Caribbean Sea, Lake Maracaibo, Orinoco River, Gulf of Guayaquil, Amazon River, São Francisco River, Lake Titicaca, Paraguay River, Paraná River, Pacific Ocean, Uruguay River, Río de la Plata, Atlantic Ocean, Gulf of San Matías, Gulf of San Jorge, Gulf of Penas, Strait of Magellan, Tierra del Fuego]

Page 63

1. tropical
2. Andes
3. tributaries
4. tidal bore
5. waterlily
6. South America
7. Atlantic

Crack the code!
Piranhas, which are native to the Amazon River, are known for their ferocious appetites.

Page 64

A. 1. f   2. a   3. h   4. b   5. e   6. g   7. d   8. c

Page 65

B. Answers will vary. Teacher check.

Page 66

A. 1. on the Churun River in the Guiana Highlands of Venezuela
2. It was named after Jimmie Angel, the first person to fly over the falls.
3. waterfall of the deepest place

B. Answers will vary. Teacher check.

Page 67

Across
3. Amazon
5. Guiana
7. Andes
8. strait

Down
1. Patagonia
2. Rainforest
4. plateau
6. Atacama

Page 71

1. Itaipú
2. Chile
3. peppers
4. 40%
5. marine iguana

Page 73

A. 1. Colombia, Ecuador, Peru and Brazil
2. Lake Maracaibo and along the Orinoco River
3. ¾
4. 2000

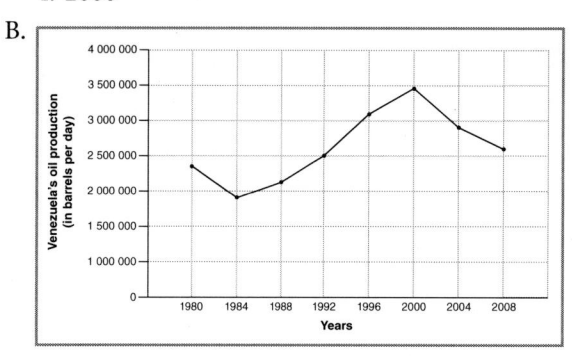

B. [Line graph titled "Venezuela's oil production (in barrels per day)" with years 1980–2008 on x-axis and values from 0 to 4,000,000 on y-axis]

Answers

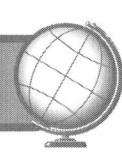

Page 75

A. 1. Paraná
   2. Paraguay
   3. seventh
   4. concrete
   5. reservoir
   6. generators
   7. water

B. 1. b 2. a 3. f 4. d 5. g 6. c 7. e

Page 76

Chile, Escondida, Atacama, pits, electricity, alloys

Page 77

1. iron
2. mercury
3. lead
4. molybdenum
5. tin
6. zinc
7. manganese

Page 79

A. 1. No   5. Yes
   2. Yes   6. No
   3. Yes   7. No
   4. No   8. Yes

B. 1. quinoa   4. Brazil nuts
   2. peppers   5. quinoa
   3. peppers   6. Brazil nuts

C. Answers will vary.

Page 81

A. 1. No   5. No
   2. Yes   6. No
   3. Yes   7. Yes
   4. Yes   8. Yes

B. Answers will vary. Teacher check.

Page 83

A. Pupils should write the letters *A, F, G, H* under 'Llama'; *D, E, I,* under 'Both'; and *B, C, J* under 'Alpaca'.

B. Answers will vary. Teacher check.

Page 85

A.

A	B	I	W	A	T	T	B	A	N	A	N	A	S	D
M	Y	B	Y	F	I	N	D	B	C	F	B	T	H	E
R	N	Q	M	T	S	L	O	W	V	M	I	E	A	M
A	N	U	M	O	R	T	W	H	A	R	E	G	L	A
Y	L	I	G	C	U	K	S	N	F	T	M	W	S	H
B	R	N	T	H	E	O	R	E	I	S	E	N	T	O
H	A	I	N	G	A	G	I	C	A	N	R	X	G	G
M	D	N	P	A	B	V	O	U	T	K	P	A	D	A
D	E	E	W	H	Q	O	X	Y	G	E	N	C	A	N
T	A	Y	U	N	E	C	I	S	A	P	I	H	V	Y
R	E	I	T	C	K	A	D	A	M	M	U	E	I	B
W	L	A	N	E	Y	D	V	E	R	S	Q	L	D	I
L	A	G	K	I	W	O	L	H	A	V	E	G	O	S
E	A	X	D	R	O	S	E	W	O	O	D	S	M	G

B. Answers will vary. Teacher check.

Page 87

A. 1. An anaconda ambushes its prey from the water and then strangles it by wrapping its own body around the prey.
   2. Anacondas, caimans, jaguars and pumas prey on capybaras.
   3. because they are very slow and helpless on the ground
   4. Piranhas will eat small fish and small animals most of the time.

B. Drawings and captions will vary. Teacher check.

Page 89

1. penguins   5. equator
2. algae   6. tortoise
3. finch
4. marine iguana

Crack the code!

In 1972, the last known surviving Pinta Island tortoise (a subspecies of the Galápagos tortoise) was taken into captivity. Sadly, he died in 2012. His name was Lonesome George.

Answers

Page 90

Across
1. Galápagos
5. quinoa
6. Chile
7. Brazil

Down
2. Paraná
3. alpacas
4. capybara
5. quinine

Page 93

1. Machu Picchu
2. a kind of martial art
3. in the Amazon Rainforest
4. soups and stews
5. 85%

Page 95

A.
1. concrete
2. Incas
3. Easter Island
4. Pacific Ocean
5. royalty
6. Corcovado Mountain
7. Machu Picchu
8. conquistadors
9. mysterious

B. Answers will vary. Teacher check.

Page 97

A.
1. stone
2. earthquakes
3. Egyptians
4. terraces
5. geometric
6. patterns
7. metalwork

B. Drawings will vary. Teacher check.

Page 99

1. couples
2. Peru
3. Argentina
4. Brazil
5. small guitar
6. Samba
7. Quechua
8. tango
9. Huayño
10. samba

Page 101

A.
1. No
2. No
3. Yes
4. No
5. Yes
6. Yes
7. No
8. Yes
9. Yes
10. No
11. No
12. No

B. Because slaves were not allowed to practise self-defence, they disguised their movements to look like a dance.

Page 102

A. Some beliefs were completely wiped out by the Spanish. Others were mixed in with the Catholic religion.

Page 103

B.
1. shamanism
2. Paraguay
3. missionaries
4. Candomblé
5. Roman Catholic
6. Brazil

Crack the code!
This religion is growing in South America today.
Protestantism

Page 105

Answers will vary. Teacher check.

Page 107

1. f   2. h   3. i   4. e   5. g   6. a   7. d   8. c   9. b

M	Y	B	P	X	H	S	A	N	D	I	D	I	G	O	L
Y	O	U	E	R	F	I	S	H	S	O	U	P	L	I	L
F	E	B	P	E	L	O	L	G	O	O	E	D	R	T	C
H	I	N	P	F	U	A	D	J	E	O	A	Y	D	A	
B	L	S	E	S	R	I	F	N	B	S	C	E	T	A	B
U	A	N	R	Y	D	U	Y	O	U	H	R	M	F	V	F
A	P	M	P	I	U	Y	I	E	N	D	P	L	I	E	
G	O	H	O	R	T	B	E	T	N	I	C	A	E	D	Z
O	T	E	T	S	A	N	C	O	C	H	O	N	A	S	G
O	A	Y	T	H	R	E	A	E	T	L	O	A	T	S	X
O	T	C	H	O	C	O	E	T	A	T	D	D	E	I	T
C	O	E	C	R	E	T	T	A	W	A	E	A	A	R	W
F	E	I	J	O	A	D	A	C	O	M	P	L	E	T	A
N	S	O	T	M	K	M	N	E	P	Q	U	A	N	K	O

Answers

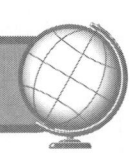

Page 108

1. February
2. lent
3. Rio de Janeiro
4. dress up in costumes and dance in the street
5. to have fun before lent
6. They build floats, design costumes, create music and practise dances.

Page 109

1. church
2. nativity
3. go to the beach
4. Ecuador
5. rollerskates
6. Greenland
7. straw
8. Argentina

Page 110

Across
2. Missionaries
4. Argentina
6. Pelé
8. Machu Picchu

Down
1. Carnaval
3. Incas
5. empanada
7. Quechua

Page 112

1. Colombia
2. Andes Mountains
3. Brazil
4. Pacific Ocean
5. Atacama Desert
6. Tierra del Fuego
7. Uruguay
8. Buenos Aires
9. Falkland Islands
10. Atlantic Ocean

Page 113

1. fourth
2. Pacific
3. Southern and Western
4. Mexico
5. Bolivia
6. oxygen
7. Nile
8. Atacama

Page 114

9. Venezuela
10. copper
11. the Amazon Rainforest
12. Llamas are wild animals.
13. Argentina
14. Catholicism
15. the Incas
16. Rio de Janeiro